Growing Up Where the Ways Crossed

William L. Bullard

ISBN 978-1-68570-324-0 (paperback)
ISBN 978-1-68570-325-7 (digital)

Christian Faith Publishing
832 Park Avenue
Meadville, PA 16335
www.christianfaithpublishing.com

Printed in the United States of America

Dedication

This writing is dedicated to my nine grandchildren in hopes that they will one day understand a little more about life in a Southern city and what it was like—the good, bad, and even some ugly times. I truly desire for them to have knowledge of bygone or forgotten experiences that occurred from my preschool to high school years.

So, Caden, Grant, Sadie, Adelaine, Finn, Eli, Violent, Charlie, and Oliver, this is for you!

I was the youngest of six children, and it is also my desire to say thank-you to my siblings: Connie, Ronnie, Joanne, Bobbie Jean, and Everett. My brother Everett has already gone to heaven. In fact, today, September 22, at this writing, my sweet sister Joanne has just left this world for heaven after having been for three weeks in her local hospital on a COVID-19-inflicted ventilator. We were praying for her complete healing, and now it is done! Joanne said just a few weeks ago to me, "Larry, I cannot wait to read your book about growing up in Waycross."

A special thanks to so many of my Waycross pals who have been lifetime friends and with whom I have shared some incredible memories.

May I say a special thanks to my wife, Ranée, and our four children—Andy, Stacey, Scott, and Emily—for allowing me to share these stories while on vacation or just sitting around the house; and, yes, we need to add those amazing in-laws, Sarah, Stephen, and Glen, who have, no doubt, endured the many repetitive moments when their father-in-law would say, "Did I ever tell you about this or that, back in the day?"

Lastly, but most of all, may I express my thankfulness to our God for allowing me to live and experience this life journey. He has brought some amazing people across my path over these last sixty-eight years!

I sincerely thank you for reading these episodes of my life in the South and specifically in Waycross! I have come to three amazing conclusions about each one of us that I would like to leave with you as you complete the reading of this memoir.

There are three ways in which the Creator of the universe knows each of us:

1. He knew us before we were ever born (Jeremiah 1:5).
2. He knows us while we are on this earth. "The eyes of the Lord are upon us" (Proverbs 5:21).
3. He knows when we will leave this earth. "For it is appointed unto men once to die" (Hebrews 9:27).

Contents

Preface

My desire is that every person who reads this book either knows Christ as his personal Savior or will come to know Him soon. My desire is that we all spend eternity together. It is doubtful that we will spend moments in heaven discussing "old times" on earth; I rather suspect we will be talking about only the new, eternal things God will introduce upon our arrival to that wonderful, new home! What a day that will be! May your life be blessed, encouraged, and edified in some way after this read. If you enjoy this little read, share it with a friend. If you do not, well, just set it on a shelf, and perhaps, in the future, someone might just pick it up, wipe off the dust, and get a glimpse of what it was like "growing up where the ways crossed."

> What man is he that feareth the Lord? Him
> shall he teach in the way that he shall choose.
> (Psalm 25:12)

God has a *way* for us. He has a *plan* for us. He has a *purpose* for us.

Introduction

The hardest part about writing this book is, where do I begin? As you go through these pages, your mind will take you to places, people, and memories of your own upbringing in your hometown. One reason I am leaving space in the margins is so you can jot down thoughts and memories that may ignite in you as you go through these pages. In a few minutes, I will begin and do my best to present correct episodes of my life growing up in the South and especially in Waycross, Georgia. I think, for the picture or the puzzle to be complete, we will go in chronological order of the houses we lived in from the first grade to the twelfth. Almost every time I would travel back through Waycross alone or with my family, undoubtedly, we had to go by and see the homes where we once resided. I would sit in front of a house, take out a pen, and write down my memories of each house. I would take pictures and remember back in the day when I played in the yard, I remembered my neighborhood friends and episodes that were associated with that specific house. I can remember, we never seemed to have a permanent home but a house. When stories are told from friends how they would go back to the homeplace, I would have to laugh and say, "Well, it is going to take us all day," because we would have to visit the ten houses we lived in from preschool to my high school graduation; and every time, I would hear "no way" from their sighs.

The choice for a book title has been rather difficult. I thought about "Down the Memory Lane," "Homesick for the South," "Remembering Waycross," and "Stories from the South." But as I studied the meaning of Waycross, I felt it very fitting to use the title *Growing Up Where the Ways Crossed*, for this was one of the original meanings of the name of the city. Waycross was a great place for ways to cross in this city of fourteen thousand! May I encourage our readers to google our city, look at the vintage pictures, read the history, and get inspired with this multifaceted city located in the southeastern region of our great state of Georgia. Historically, Waycross was put on the maps for the railroads and the Okefenokee Swamp. There is so much I would love to put in this writing about the history of our city, but we have some amazing researchers who have written great articles about the founding days of this wonderful place!

Sometimes I think, why didn't they tell us that a 1966 Super Sport Chevrolet would be selling in Scottsdale, Arizona, for more than $100,000? Why didn't someone tell me that my first car, the two-toned 1964 Comet, which I bought for only $300, would one day be worth more than $50,000? How about that 1969 Dodge Super Bee that one of my friends owned and picked me up in almost every day in the twelfth grade would one day be worth more than $100,000? We just did not know! What if we had been able to buy a few of those cars and put them in a warehouse for fifty years? That would have been a good retirement benefit! Well, we did not know, and if we had known, how many of us could have come up with enough money to buy one or two to put in that warehouse? So in life, we must let some things go!

Have you ever heard the words "there is no place like home"? Of course, we all have heard and used those words. We all use that expression from time to time. The truth is, we all are making memories today and every day. Our children that are grown are already saying, "Back in the day, we did this" and "we did that" or "remember when"? The older they become, the words "there is no place like home" will be part of their vernacular. May I say about Waycross, there is no place like home. When I say this, I truly am speaking about the city, not the home where I grew up. The reason is we lived in ten houses in twelve years!

Just like your parents, our mom and dad set the pace for our thinking in so many areas of life. My parents have been in heaven for many years now; it is still an honor for me to purchase flowers, take a drive to the Baxley, Georgia, area and visit my parents' graves. I receive immense joy taking the time to remember my upbringing with my wonderful parents. I sure do miss them! My mother honored her parents with flowers on their grave sites, so I learned to do that from her. We learned so much from our parents. If your parents have already passed away, I am sure you miss them as we miss our parents!

May I respectfully write these episodes of my life in the South with discretion and honor. I may leave some names out but not intentionally, for I never want to overlook someone who touched my life. I will only include the first name of persons mentioned in the stories; and in some situations, I will not mention a name but just say "a friend." If you are from Waycross, you will know the streets and places mentioned. If you grew up in another city, memories will surface of your hometown during this era. Each one of us has a history! Okay, dear friend, let's go for a little drive down memory lane!

Mary Street

I was born in 1952 in Macon, Georgia. My family moved from Macon to Baxley, Georgia. From Baxley, we moved to Waycross! The year was 1955. My family moved from Baxley to Waycross in my preschool year. Dad had been out of the navy for a few years and had begun his career in the grocery business. If I accurately recall, he worked for the Piggly Wiggly food chain in Macon, and then also in Baxley. My mother was great at customer service, and her talent was serving in the cafeteria at the local school, restaurants, and bakeries. I vividly remember, for a brief period, her working at a tomato factory in Baxley that memory of the smell of tomatoes stayed with me for a long time. I'm thankful that I had a mother who knew how to work, help, and loved to serve people, but that tomato factory was absolutely the worst smell in the world!

The move to Waycross took us to Mary Street near Isabella Elementary School. I was not in school at the time, but my twin sister and brother, Connie and Ronnie, attended Isabella for their first and second grades. I can remember living upstairs in a small apartment right across the street from my future eighth-grade school classroom. Remember the eighth-grade school? Remember Isabella School? It is just one block over from the most incredible Mary Street Park, and down the street from the St. Joseph Catholic School. I remember that the park had a great ball field, green grass, lots of trees, and a famous merry-go-round ride that would make you so dizzy. I, like probably most kids, can remember getting off that merry-go-round, feeling so dizzy that I could hardly walk. I think that was one of the reasons I grew up not wanting to ride the rides at the Waycross Fair that would give you that round-and-round, dizzy sensation. I don't think I am alone, for many probably had that phobia. As I am writing this, I can recall that sensation from the merry-go-round! Mary Street Park was a wonderful place to play, and I believe it has had various names throughout the years. In recent days, it was dedicated as Pernell Roberts Park, and a memorial was placed there in his honor.

I remember how we lived in the upstairs apartment of that huge, white house. If I recall correctly, we had to climb a rather high outdoor staircase to get to our apartment located on the second story. As I look back, it must have been a real challenge for Mom and Dad to bring groceries up those steps. As kids, we really don't think about those things. But later in life, it makes us appreciate what our parents went through to take care of their families.

Ronnie and Connie would go down those steps every day headed to Isabella School located one block away. Mom must have kept me during the day, or she hired a nanny to take care of me until my brother and sister got home from school. It does seem like I remember going down to the park quite often, so perhaps I did have a day sitter.

Recently, I rode by the first house we lived in on Mary Street; and it still looks pretty much like I remember. Right across the street was the school we would attend in the eighth grade. As kids, didn't we enjoy playing in the yard in the dirt? Nothing like taking our shoes off and getting dirt between our toes. Wasn't it fun going in the yard and digging a hole with a little shovel? I was thinking recently about something interesting about those days: I never could figure out how we could dig a hole and then put the same dirt back in the hole; but we never seemed to have enough dirt to fill the hole back up! How does that happen? I think sometimes about stuff that I really do not understand, but I guess all of us do. Another random thought: I don't know why eating a bowl of cereal was so good; and then the best was yet to come—drinking the milk from the bowl! It may not be proper today, but it sure was good back in the day!

Walker Street

F or some reason, we moved to the Walker Street area in 1956. This house leaves me with little memory and events, except it was next door to a famous movie star named Pernell Roberts. Being a child and not knowing much about movie stars, I just remembered Dad and Mom saying a famous person would come and visit his parents who lived close to us. Wow! Later, we learned about the TV show, *Bonanza*, and the reality hit us. Oh, *that* was who that was. Years have passed, and now the park down the street that I mentioned earlier has a very nice marker with his name. If you take a moment to google Waycross, you will find that quite a few celebrities spent their early years in Waycross.

Let's take a drive "across town" (that is how we would say it) toward Wacona Elementary School. We will drive a good bit down State Street toward Jamestown, and you will see the school. Look for the structure that looks like the front of the Alamo.

State Street

We moved from Walker Street to State Street, just a few miles from Wacona Elementary. I was about to enter the first grade, and it was like my life was about to begin. I can remember my first-grade teacher, Mrs. Cavender. No doubt, many of you that attended Wacona Elementary remembered this wonderful teacher who had a heart for her students. I think she knew she had a challenge on her hands with me for she would invite me (with my parents' permission) to come to her house and enjoy the outdoors. Maybe it was because I seemed to have a challenging time paying attention in class or some other reason. She probably had a good prayer life and would pray, "Lord, please help Larry to pay attention in class." I am not sure, but I think I had (and still have) a touch of ADD, ADHD, and a little OCD!

So it was 1957, and I am not sure why, but we moved again all the way across town to State Street. Across the street from that house were the railroad tracks, and just a few miles down the street was our new school. Our mother got a job at the school cafeteria, and I will never forget the smell of those yeast rolls! They were so good! My mind takes me back to that long walk in the first grade to get to school. I remember my siblings, and I would have to walk in front of an old house that was set back off the road. Many stories were told of a witch who lived there. I am not sure if that was true, but when I look back over that experience, it reminded me of the *Wizard of Oz*. On the way to school, we were always looking for a witch riding a broom to fly over us. It is funny how stories are told and how easily kids believe those stories!

An extremely sweet memory about our mother when we lived on State Street: from time to time, we would have tramps come up to our house. These tramps were homeless men who traveled from town to town on the trains. When the train would come through town, the tramps would seem to know exactly where to go for something to eat. Mama would make up a batch of homemade biscuits and sausage. She would wrap them up in a towel and place them in a pan at the backdoor for the tramps to have something to eat. I don't know how they found their way to our house, but not long ago, while visiting the San Diego Model Railroad Museum, I learned that the "tramp community," as you might describe it, had a unique communication system in which they would use various markings along the way to relay important information to one another. One particular marking (placed on the home itself) would be to point out who in the town might be friendly or sympathetic toward tramps. I don't recall noticing any special markings on our house, but who knows? From my perspective, hopefully, these poor, destitute men were thankful for our mom who did her best to care. At the same time, Mom was extremely cautious and would lock the doors for our safety. I really think, even as a child, I learned something about hospitality, love, and concern for others from seeing my mother's caring heart. Thanks, Mom! Let's go down the street and go across the tracks to find Atwood Street.

Atwood Street

For some reason, after my first grade, we moved from State Street to Atwood Street, which was just a few miles down the road and across the tracks. I believe, the year was 1959. I think, if you ride by now, you will see a beautiful home that has had extra rooms added. My dad had purchased a blue, cool-looking Studebaker that had front headlight areas shaped like rockets! Remember those rocket rides for a dime you could ride in front of stores? That is exactly what that car resembled. When Dad was coming home from his work at the grocery store, we knew exactly when to go stand at the entrance of the long driveway; and sure enough, Dad would pull in, and we would hop on the rocket and ride up to the house. For a kid, that was big. It was one thing to ride on the car but also special to spend that time with Dad! I remember, across the street was an exceedingly kind family. I can still see my neighbor in my mind's eye, standing up and riding upon a huge lawn mower, which was a new and unusual phenomenon in that day!

Let me tell you about an episode that happened on Atwood that left a scar on my right hand. I will never forget that day when my sister "scared the fire" out of my brother and me. Ronnie and I were in the bathtub playing with our plastic boats and pretending the miniature plastic men were diving off the waterspout (and I am sure, many of you remember those childhood moments). Connie sneaked up the stairs, began making those "whoo" and eerie sounds that we all remember. When we heard those noises, it did not sound like my sister's voice. We believed it was a ghost; after all, we had not moved too far from that house where we thought a witch lived. We got so scared; both of us jumped out of the tub, grabbed a towel, and down the stairs we went. In our fear, we ran across the street to a neighbor's house, but they were not home. I think, by this time, my brother had grabbed my towel. And there I was, standing in my yard, naked as a jaybird. I was only in the second grade, but I was embarrassed, scared, and by this time, angry. Connie had locked the door, and we were now standing on the porch. I looked up, trying to peek in the little glass windowpane on the door but could not reach high enough to see. I did not know what to do, so I hit the glass with my right hand, busted the window, and got my sister's attention. My hand was bleeding, and soon we found ourselves inside, bandaging up the wound. Of course, it healed, but I was left with a scar to remind me of our sister-inflicted terror! I am sure the readers of this story had similar episodes growing up. That one was not a fun one. By the way, my sister did ask for us to forgive her, and we did!

Around the corner was a neat family that owned horses. Every year, they would ride their horses in the downtown Waycross parade. By the way, some of the best parades were those Waycross parades. Remember the Shriners riding the scooters and throwing candy? It seemed like every business made a float, and they were all so colorful, creative and fun! Back in the day, it was like people took so much pride in their town and welcomed opportunities to be involved in community events. I loved those downtown parades!

A few days ago, I took a ride by Wacona Elementary and saw my first- and second-grade building still standing in the back of the property. One of most exciting words I recall in those early years of school was *recess*! Remember? The boys would make straw houses for the girls, and it seemed the girls really took to the boys that were creative with building rooms, hallways, and playing like they were real houses. I had already moved around quite a bit in Waycross, so it did not take much time for me to put my imagination to work when designing the floor plans for those straw houses. But all good things had to end; so after recess, we would head back to class. My second-grade teacher was Mrs. Denton, and I can tell you, all of us boys thought she was some kind of "purty."

On occasion, I think about the teachers that invested their lives in us as kids, and I hope we all stay grateful for their investment! For some reason, probably because of my dad's job, we decided to move across town again. So you go down State Street back to town, and just a few streets over from Harris Supermarket, you will find Grove Avenue.

Grove Avenue

The year was 1960, and we have moved to Grove Avenue. No longer did we live on a street, we had moved to an avenue. I can remember, I was somewhat excited because we seemed to be moving a little closer to the city. I love the country, and I love way-out in the country, but there was just something kind of neat about moving closer to town. In my opinion, every area of Waycross had wonderful people, and every person had their wonderful families.

Soon, and seemingly quickly, I met some great friends. Up until this move, probably because I was so young, I cannot remember having many friends. Now, in this new home, I thought it was incredible to be surrounded by boys my own age! Next door was Danny.

Behind us lived Jimmy. Around the corner was Marion. Down the street was Troy. A few blocks away was R. L. Where were all the girls?

This chapter of my life was a really fun time for me. The days, weeks, and months ahead turned out to be great in so many ways. Mama was working at the Bluebird restaurant on State Street, and my dad was one of the store managers at Harris Market on State. We now lived only a few blocks from their workplaces, so that was good for them. That may be why we moved to that location. I did not want to forget to say, my mother later worked at Tuten's Bakery and Barger's Bakery. Of course, it was fun visiting her workplace with the doughnuts, cakes, pies, and those white wedding finger cookies with pecans. Remember? I think they were called lady fingers and were so amazingly good with a glass of cold milk! I can taste them right now while I am writing this book.

Get yourself a cup of coffee, for this chapter may take a few minutes. Behind our house on Grove Avenue was a carport. Dad said, "Let's build a clubhouse on top of it. We were all for it! So Dad located the wood and the metal and began the project.

By this time, the neighborhood boys and I had become friends and did everything together. We rode bikes (I had to borrow one); played ball; laughed; acted crazy, like boys do; and had a blast. I mentioned these friends at the beginning of this chapter. Danny lived next door, and his family owned a printing shop downtown; they are still in business after all these years. I can still see in my mind a sweet lady that worked with Danny's family named Hattie. She was tough and sweet at the same time. I recall, on occasion, she fixed snacks for us boys when we would stop long enough to eat something. Isn't it amazing how long boys can play outside? Do girls do the same? I am sure. Danny is a good friend to this day!

Marion lived next to Danny. I had to ask Marion a few years ago to forgive me. I don't know why, but I shot him in the arm with my Daisy BB gun. Why would a kid do that to his friend? Marion and I are still great friends to this day. Jimmy lived behind us. Well, you'd go from my backyard into his backyard, and we would stop to pick some muscadines off his parents' grapevines. After fifty years, I was able to locate Jimmy, and we talked on the phone recently.

Living miles and miles away has a tendency, literally, to distance friends, doesn't it?

John lived next door, but he was older. Sonny was older; he was Danny's brother. Three boys came in for the summer months and stayed with their grandmother, Mrs. Garrett; I believe they were Dickie, Joe, and Jim. I can remember, they were awesome baseball players.

Down the street a little way was Troy. He lived by Dad's Grocery across from the tobacco warehouse. Around the corner, just one block away, lived another great friend named Tony. Close by, lived Rosemary; she played with Connie. Down the street, a little farther, was the McNeal family; they owned a lawn mower business on State Street. Their shop was the place to go and sell pecans that we gathered from the local yards. I would go to a friend's house and ask if I could pick up pecans in their yard and sell them. People were so kind and gracious! I do remember one girl that lived in the neighborhood, and she was a beauty. I think a few of us fought over her a few times! She lived on Riverside Drive, so it was far enough away not to interfere much with our clubhouse.

Some of these great friends would get together every week for our club meeting. They were Danny, Marion, Jimmy, and Troy. My sister and brother, Connie and Ronnie, and these close associates, aka club members, would meet every Saturday for our meeting in the garage clubhouse. We had to bring ten cents or a soft drink bottle cap for dues.

If you didn't bring your dues, you possibly would have punishment. I can recall one of the club members had to be tied to a clothesline (for just a few minutes) because he forgot his dues. Those are just the kind of things boys did back then—innocent fun. Wow, I can see in my mind's eye right now those gatherings in the ole clubhouse, climbing up the plywood steps and attending our weekly meeting. I wish I could remember our conversations. Imagine what kids our age would meet and talk about. Later on, when I saw Spanky and Our Gang, I could not help but think we were much like those kids!

I also remember that muscadine vine in Jimmy's yard that I mentioned a few minutes ago. We would eat until we were full of those juicy grapes. I never knew what his mother thought about all of us, but I would think she might not have appreciated us eating all her grapes. I imagine a whole lot of forgiveness was granted to us in those days for we "knew not what we were doing," so to speak! Jimmy did not stop us, so I guess it was all good.

Marion would sometimes tell me that his mother was a little upset with me. I would ask him why, and usually, it had something to do with something I had done that I should not have done. I think many times I had to ask her to forgive me. I don't know, maybe as boys, we also picked on each other so much that our own parents got annoyed with us. What do you think?

Can you remember how Halloween was represented with fun, laughter, food, popcorn balls, candy apples, and all the other stuff? Our neighborhood seemed to go all out for it. It really was in a great time in the neighborhood. One of the scariest Halloween nights was when two of the older guys, John and Sonny, put sheets over their heads like ghosts and scared the fire out of us all. I am talking about screaming, yelling, and running to get away!

Back to our club, my sister, Connie, was our treasurer. I cannot remember which girls she asked to join the club. One might have been Marion's sister. Honestly, if a girl was smart, she would not have joined because our gang was always getting into something. I think my brother, Ronnie, and a few of his buddies were always attacking us or doing something out of the ordinary but not sure. Connie kept a weekly ledger of our dues. Our names were written down; and out to the side, she would record if we were paid up or not. This was a good learning tool for us to pay our bills on time. One of the things we seemed to enjoy doing was burying stuff in the yard. I can remember burying bottles, cola caps, jars, etc.

An amazing thing happened in real time as I was writing this book. Over sixty years have passed, and I went by to see the house on Grove Avenue. The lady who lives there now greeted me, and we chatted a few minutes about that house where I lived for a time. I told her how we buried bottles and stuff. She said, "Are you kidding?" She went in her house and brought me two little bottles she had dug up, and she graciously gave them to me. I was not sure, but they could

GROWING UP WHERE THE WAYS CROSSED

have been some of the ones the club buried back in the day. What great memories with those great childhood friends on Grove Avenue! By the way, I told her I thought we had buried a jar of money (our dues) somewhere by the big ole tree next to where the clubhouse was located. She was kind, got excited, and said that if she found it, she would call and give it to me. Would not that be so awesome if she found that jar of dues? Now, that would be a storybook tale for sure!

As of this writing, two of those dear friends, Troy and Tony, are now in heaven and are missed by all of us. Later in life, both Troy and Tony asked Jesus into their lives to be their personal Savior; their lives really made a difference to encourage others in this life journey. For some reason, as a child, I was shy to have a conversation with the pastor of the church we attended, Central Baptist Church on Brunel. When he came to see me one day at home, I hid under the kitchen/dining room table and would not come out. Can you imagine? But if we fast-forward the tape, there came a superspecial moment at one of our high school reunions in Waycross. Tony and I had become pastors after all those crazy years growing up. We were invited to speak at the Second Baptist Church in Waycross the next morning after the reunion. We looked out in the congregation and saw about three pews full of our friends from high school. It was an awesome service, and we got to worship together! It was rather amazing how it all happened, and Tony and I got the honor to share how the Lord has changed our lives. This should give everybody hope! I truly have believed, all these years, if God can change a sinner like me, then He can change anybody! A few years ago, when Troy went to heaven, it was an honor to speak at his life celebration service. Wow, the memories linger in my heart about these amazing friends. Thank God for heaven, for one day we will see each other again!

One of the greatest fun times in the neighborhood was the Wiffle ball game on Quarterman Street—absolutely the best fun ever! The road was dirt, and we would make bases in the road. Now when it rained, we also had a big mess on our hands; but then, we changed into our rain clothes and played in the mud. Fun! When the word got out, friends came from everywhere, riding their bikes. You could hear them coming with their playing cards attached by clothespins to the wheel spokes; it sounded like a modern-day Bike Week at Daytona or Sturgis. It just came to me; I think we were called the Grove Avenue Gang. I am not sure, but I just know it was a great chapter in our lives!

You can see rather clearly that Grove Avenue was a place of immeasurable memories. Think about it, we had our own authentic club in the neighborhood, and it was incredible! I know this was a rather long chapter, but so much happened in that house on Grove Avenue.

Stay with me, we are going to move just one block away. That's right—one block. Before I tell you about the next move, let's take some time and talk about our elementary school that was literally two houses away from my house on Grove Avenue. I really wish the school was standing today, for the memories are fascinating. Let's go across the street and remember...

Quarterman Street School

How could any of us forget Quarterman Street School, the wooden benches built around the trees where we could sit and talk to friends and maybe even a young girlfriend that wanted to sit and chat? Remember the square dancing class later in the seventh grade? The Halloween festivals were incredible with the teachers hanging a sheet over a wire and giving us a fishing pole with a clothespin over the wire; you would catch a toy every time. How about the huge fire escape to slide down for a nickel or a dime? It seemed like the homemade fudge with pecans was incredible; it was the kind that was a little crispy and crunchy. Know what I mean? Every room was decorated, and every teacher got involved to give Quarterman Street School students great memories! I ride by that property every now and then, park my car, and remember those days. It was a large, two-story, redbrick, foursquare building with wooden floors.

My third-grade teacher was Mrs. Moses. I had Mrs. Murphy for both fourth-grade and sixth-grade. Mrs. Van was my fifth-grade teacher, and Mrs. Justice was my seventh-grade teacher. One of the things I think most of us all wanted to do was go outside and clean the erasers; do you agree? So it was exciting when the teacher called my name to go clean the erasers. I found out later that it really was a form of discipline. I sure did go outside many times for some reason. I truly thought I was being rewarded. Did your teacher ever call your name and say, "Please stop that, or please listen?" Mrs. Murphy was a sweet soul, and very smart. I think she liked my being in her class; or maybe she treated all of us the same way, but she always made you feel special. I must say, one of the things I did not like to do was getting her water from the cooler in the hallway because she wore bright red lipstick, and her lip marks were always left on the glass. But that was okay, she was worth it. I really think that was where we got the words "yuuu" or "yuck."

Thanks for going to school for a minute with me. So back to our moving episodes. Just down Quarterman Street, one block and turn left, you will find our next house on Alice Street.

Alice Street

Nineteen sixty-two was a move we would never forget. Again, for some reason, we found ourselves packed up and moving to a small, two-bedroom house on Alice Street. It seemed like our houses were getting smaller; or else, we all were just getting bigger! In many ways, this move was awkward and confusing to my childish mind. Why in the world did we pack up move just one block away? Ever the optimist, I did not dwell long on this thought; instead, I chose to consider the happy fact that I could continue going to Quarterman Street School and having those friends that I had on Grove Avenue while adding a few more! I am sure you can imagine, but just one block away would begin a new journey of exploration and added friends. You never forsook or forgot those in the last neighborhood, you just added some new ones. Before it was over, you had many friends for sure (unless you made some enemies along the way). To me, it was awesome! I am sure we did not use the word "awesome" back in the day, but whatever word we used, it was a good one!

Heading into the fifth grade, we no longer needed the neighborhood clubhouse. Now our attention was more focused on school, homework, sports, and a little more (but not much) toward girls in our classes at school. I think I was only in one real fight in grade school. I was coming home from school, and after a boy threatened in class to beat me up, he was waiting for me at the street corner. He had his buddies with him, and I remember being alone. He threw his books down and came after me, swinging and hitting me. To be honest, I am not sure if I even got a punch in. The only other time I got in a fight was years later in San Diego, while I was in the navy. At this time, I did not know the Lord in a personal way, and I had gone to the Enlisted Men's Club. Afterward, I was walking alone when, out of nowhere, came another sailor from behind the bushes. It was a déjà vu moment for me! The guy immediately reminded me (in looks) of the boy that came after me in grade school. I am not bragging, but I remember some other sailors having to pull me off the other sailor. Gratefully, that was the last physical fight I was ever in.

Alice Street was the house we lived in when the news came on our television about President Kennedy being shot in Dallas, Texas. I can remember how it shocked and scared all of us. It was a sad day in our country to soon watch the funeral service and see his flag-draped casket carried on a horse-drawn caisson to Arlington Memorial Cemetery. That was a sobering day.

Today, when I go back and see the street signs on the streets where we lived, so many of them look so short, but when we were kids, they looked so tall! Know what I mean? So here we were in a new place, new neighborhood, and the process started all over again, learning the neighborhood friends. Dad was working at Harris Market on State Street, and Mom was working at the Bluebird restaurant not far from our house. I really loved going up to the store to visit Dad from time to time. I also loved going to see our mom at the restaurant; she would always provide us with pie or dessert.

My dad would use his creativity to make the sale signs, which hung in the windows to advertise the weekly specials—signs like "Hamburger Meat: 45 cents per pound" or "10 Pounds Potatoes: 39 cents." I can remember how neat and straight his letters and numbers were on the market signs. Dad taught us in those early years to go the extra mile for the customer. I remember he would always greet the customer with a smile even when he was not feeling that great. I also can remember him saying, "Yes, sir," and "Yes, ma'am," out of respect for the customers. To this day, it is embedded in my character to emulate what I heard and saw him do with the customers. I am sure those of you reading this can identify with me and probably do the same! The customer is not always right, but it is okay to help them think they are right. Just smile and keep doing what you are supposed to do! No business can be successful without them!

That Ford Falcon will pop up a few times in this book. We did not have air-conditioning, but when the windows were down, who needed air-conditioning? Our dad let us know that soon we would be going on vacation to Key West. What? We have never been that far before—never. What car will we take? Please, not the 1961 Falcon! Yep, and plans were being made!

We packed up and headed to Key West for a short vacation, and we soon wished we had that air-conditioning for sure. The truth, if you did not have something, you really did not miss it. Wow, that trip was a hot one! It seemed like we traveled a week to get there. I remember the heat, the gnats, the mosquitoes, and being on the side of the road, changing a tire. Flat tires on the main highway to Key West were a challenge, and that tire iron was the lifesaver! Back in the day, the spare tire was the same size as the regular tires, so we did not have to put a little doughnut tire on the Falcon.

You will have a hard time believing this episode, but it happened. One afternoon, while living on Alice Street, Dad said, "Larry, let's go out to Swamp Road and shoot the new .22 rifle."

I was excited to go for sure. So here we go, just Dad and me.

"Now, Larry, you sit in the back seat, put the rifle on the seat, and when I see something to shoot, you take the rifle off the safety, place the rifle out the back window, and I will tell you when and what to shoot."

That was all fine, but when Dad told me to put it out the window, I got so excited. I turned the safety off, lifted the gun toward the window, accidentally pulled the trigger, and fired the rifle through the driver's seat—yep, missing my dad's buttocks about two or three inches! It scared him so much. He pulled over, knowing that he had been shot. Parents, it might be a better idea to *not* try doing this like we did! God's mercy was in play for us, for I could have easily shot my dad. Be safe! It makes me think how many kids must have learned to shoot a rifle or pistol out on Swamp Road!

Then came the rattlesnake episode! As we were driving that same day of the seat shooting, Dad came across a snake that appeared to be about six-feet long stretched out across that sandy Swamp Road. He got out of the car, looked in the trunk, got a long broom handle, and shooed the snake off the road. He had courage, but the old saying was, "If you ran over a big snake like that, it would wrap around the tire and could get you later." Since that day. I was never fond of snakes.

Looking back over some of those early events in life, in some ways (now that I've seen the movie), I felt like a young Forrest Gump! Times were simple and innocent. We never knew what life was going to give us, but it was packed with plenty of emotional challenges! When I look back over the Alice Street saga, it seemed to be a place that had much heartache, trauma, and a little more drama or, should we say, maturing. Keep reading, and I think you will find the information about the Goat Man rather interesting, for he was a real man with a legendary story.

The Legendary Goat Man

The Alice Street residence seemed to create many events that left me wanting to talk about for years to come. One episode was the Goat Man. Remember him? He would travel from town to town with a small herd of goats. Dad knew where he was living in Waycross and took me to see him. I didn't know until later that he was known throughout the South. When we got to the place he was living, we saw metal scraps, wood, supplies, tools, and of course, the goats. The Goat Man would make his money building things and selling them along his way. It was incredible how smart and creative he really was in his own way.

It was Christmas morning, and standing by the Christmas tree was a two-tone, beautiful, used-but-new-to-me, blue-with-chrome-fenders bicycle. Where did my parents get it? You guessed it—from the Goat Man. I was so pumped to get a bicycle for Christmas! The bike was a Western Flyer, complete with the metal sticker on front, and I was sure it could fly! One nice thing about Alice Street is that it had a pretty steep incline going from Butler down to Riverside, perfect for getting up speed on a bicycle. I got on my bike on that cool, Christmas morning, heading down the street. I am not sure what happened, but I lost control and hit a pole. After the impact, the wheel was bent, the handlebars were crooked, and I noticed there was blood. I felt my mouth; my front tooth was broken in half, and blood was coming from my gums. Not good! Oh no, now we would have to see a dentist!

My First Dentist Visit

Mom and Dad saved up, and soon they made an appointment with Dr. Eleazer in the Bunn Building. Who likes to go to the dentist? Not me! I don't think I'd ever been! Soon, I was greeted by Mrs. Eleazer in the office; and off to the dental chair I would go. It seemed like everything in the room was green. I received what was called a root canal and also had to have a crown. It was rather challenging for a child to lose one of his permanent teeth so young. That bike ride turned out to be an expensive ride on Christmas morning! Mom was so sweet; she made a down payment and made payments every week until the balance with Dr. Eleazer was paid. You know something kinda crazy? Years later, Dr. Eleazer's daughter, Janie, became my girlfriend in the twelfth grade. I think I told her that story a few times about my childhood visit to see her dad. I know I told him a few times, and he also remembered the incident. A few years ago, before Dr. and Mrs. Eleazer passed, I was going through town and stopped by to see them. We laughed and shared some great moments. He took me fishing when I was a teenager, and I think that trip was planned to have a conversation about my dating his daughter. It was a fun trip. Another ironic thing happened; later, I became a dental technician in the navy, and after the navy, I really wanted to go to dental school in Charleston, South Carolina. But life's plans changed!

Peewee Football

It seemed like yesterday! Playing football in the Peewee League was such a memorable time. We played most of our games behind Alice Street Elementary, and I had a wonderful coach named Bill Strickland. It was a great experience! Coach Bill would say, "Larry, for every touchdown you score, I will give you piece of peppermint candy."

Truthfully, I think I was the only kid on the team that did not have any cleats, and I had to play barefoot. The good thing about that is you can run fast barefoot, especially if you're skinny and short! That little piece of candy was a motivator for me; I mean, it stirred me up inside! It seemed like the favorite play for me was the old double reverse, and I played in the backfield as a halfback. The quarterback got the ball and gave it off to the other halfback. He came running around my direction and handed it off to me. It would really confuse the defense, and in one game, I scored three touchdowns, got three pieces of candy, and had the humble honor for the team to pick me up and put me on their shoulders. That candy was delicious!

To this day, I appreciate Coach Bill and those on that awesome team. Don't ever underestimate the power that one word of encouragement, or one piece of candy, can do for a kid!

Cub Scouts and Boy Scouts

I recall wearing the blue uniform for the Cub Scouts and the green uniform for the Boy Scouts. The meetings were such a fun time with our cub leader and our scout master—the oaths, dues, united spirit, and those summer camping jamborees. I also recall learning to cook eggs and bacon over the fire and then making those fabulous pancakes. May we never take for granted those who poured into our lives as young men and women in the scouting programs. Character training, teaching of values and vision are vital qualities needed, and many fortunate young people acquired them in the scouts. Many went on to become Eagle Scouts, but I stopped short. My wife's brother, Michael Webb, became an Eagle Scout, and we could see how it gave him such an incredible foundation and passion for the outdoors. To all you Scouts, God bless you!

The Day the Back Seat Burned Up

Remember those funny but not so funny things that happened in your childhood? One afternoon, Dad was driving our 1961 Falcon and smoking one of those Pall Mall cigarettes. I never liked smoking, but it appeared that so many did in the day. It seemed like everywhere you went, someone was smoking a Lucky Strike, Kool, Pall Mall, or would make their own from Prince Albert tobacco. I am not for smoking. It is dangerous, and it does cause cancer! If you are a young person reading this, please never start smoking; it is one of the worst habits you could ever begin in your life. Quit before you ever start!

So my dad was driving down the street, threw his cigarette butt out the window, and because the back window was down, it landed in the back seat! Soon he started smelling smoke and then saw some fire. He had burned the back seat up with a stinking cigarette butt! Did we get the seat fixed? Nope. For the duration of the '61 Falcon, when we went for a ride, we had to put metal chairs in the back, and off we would go, all five of us, headed to Dairy Queen. Simple huh? Crazy? That was the way it was! One thing for sure, our dad was creative; we could have just sat on the floorboard! I had forgotten this story until my sister, Connie, reminded me in recent days. We laughed so hard together, thinking about how things were back in the day. Imagine, no seat belts, and then, of all things, driving down the road with the kids sitting in metal chairs in the back seat. Parents today would not *even* have that kind of thought, or maybe they would! I am glad we had a dad that let nothing stop him from taking us to Dairy Queen or some other place! Oh, can I mention, how did our parents drink those Coca-Colas in two swallows? That amazed me!

Remembering Those Things
I Heard as a Child

- Daddy does make the rules, and mother helps us keep them.
- Don't wear your hat inside.
- No slamming doors in the house
- We will eat, but we need to say the blessing first.
- If you spill the coffee in the saucer, drink the coffee in the saucer.
- If you pee in the bed, don't get so mad. You can play marbles in the perfect pee ring.
- When you play marbles, you need a good cat-eyed marble.
- When your hair is touching your ear, we need to go to the barbershop.
- If you use a glass, rinse it out afterward.
- No fishing on Sunday, cutting grass on Sunday, or washing clothes on Sunday.
- Stores are closed on Sunday, so no work on Sunday.
- If you used the car, put the same amount of gas back in that you used.
- Take your shoes off at the door please.
- Wash your heels, not just your feet. Wash behind your ears, or corn might grow.
- We will say, "Yes, sir," and "Yes, ma'am," in and out of this house.
- Take 10 percent of what you make, and give it to God; this is called the tithe.

- If you are going to have a job, then work hard and do not be late.
- You are no better than anyone, and no one is better than you.

More Sayings We Heard as Kids

Each of us can recall the sayings from our grandparents, aunts, uncles, cousins, brothers, sisters, and parents, such as the following:

- "Watch out for the snakes." To this day, I am not very fond of them. Yes, God created them, but I am not sure for what purpose. Notice, they did not say to watch out for dogs, cats, mice, spiders, wasps, but only snakes!
- "Not too close to the well." My aunt would say that so much when we would visit her house in the country. My uncle would draw water from the well; and every time I helped him, I stretched my arm out to not get too close.
- "Children, don't jump on the bed." I can guarantee, every person reading this jumped on the bed. Remember this line from a poem, "That's what you get for jumping on the bed."
- "Be sure to say your prayers." I can remember not ever wanting to close an eye before saying, "Now I lay me down to sleep."

Let's reflect and be thankful for those sayings and many more. I think they were motivated by love, and that love wanted us to be safe and cared for. May we be thankful for those days and the words.

A Good Word about Other Neighborhoods in Waycross

Waycross was a town of diversity and appreciation for people— all people. While we were all young, growing up in that small Southern town, none of us realized what social dynamics were taking place throughout our city. It was not until we reached the middle school years that we truly got to meet people from all the other areas of town. Our city was indeed divided, but most of us young kids neither knew nor understood that reality. By the time I reached junior high, I began to recognize that segregation and distinctly diverse sections of town existed in Waycross, a situation which, I am certain, was present in most towns as well. There were three schools available in the 1960s: Center High School for our city's black students, Waycross High School for white students living within the city limits, and Ware County High School for students living beyond the city limits. If you fast-forward the tape, all three schools have now come together as *one*, and today it is called Ware County High School. The county in which Waycross is found is, of course, Ware County.

No section of the city was any better than another section, and no one was any better than another. Socially and racially speaking, throughout America, cities and towns were divided. I remember how one day it seemed to all change here in Waycross. I think it happened while I was attending Quarterman Street School in the sixth or seventh grade. Social walls began to come down throughout the city, and there were no more racial divisions within the school system. I remember liking that. For even though I did not have a personal relationship with the Lord at that time in my life, I did have respect for all people! Plus, it gave me the opportunity of meeting new friends!

In truth, I believe there is only one true race, the *human race*! We are one United States; and when a nation is divided, it will not stand. If a city is divided, it will not stand either. I strongly believe, a city must have leaders who are wise, creative, smart, keen, professional, and totally synchronized. These leadership qualities are vital in order for a city or town to grow and have the blessings of God upon city officials, government officials, educational officials, and residents!

Fun Times Just Being Kids

- Throwing rocks up in the dark night air just to see the bats chase them under the streetlights
- Putting playing cards in the spokes of our bikes so we could sound like a motorcycle gang going down the street or on the sidewalk
- Placing a cardboard box in the yard, putting some bread under it, tying a piece of long string to a stick, propping up the box, and waiting for that hungry bird to come by— you may wait for some time, but I have experienced the catching of a bird only to let it go after we caught that little thing.
- Playing hopscotch on a sidewalk with chalk—everybody loved that game.
- The game "drop the handkerchief" seemed to be a favorite, especially when we had five to eight people playing. It was just a fun pastime.

On the Other Side of the Tracks

Let me so honestly say that when I was growing up, I felt like I lived on the "other side of the tracks," so to speak. In simple terms, when those words were used, it meant that we did not live in a community where there was much money, and we didn't quite feel like we matched up to other people's standards of living. I honestly never believed into that thinking! In fact, today, my thinking about that statement is quite simple: It is a myth. Good night, my friend. In Waycross we have so many railroad tracks. We *all* lived across the tracks! Wow, I had friends in every section of the city, and I liked them, and they liked me—I think so anyway! So rather than living like that and having that kind of mindset, I would tell people, "Just get over that kind of thinking." I had a daddy and mama that taught us, "No one is better than you, and you are no better than anyone."

You are what you are, and God had something to do with your design and heritage. If God wanted to place you in another home, He could have easily designed it for you. But God gave you and me the parents that He gave us, and we should live our lives to the fullest measure with thankfulness and gratitude. I am so convinced that many people in this life's journey need to get over what they have been under! Stop blaming this person or the next. Stop criticizing and tearing down others. Hold up your head and say, "I was created by the God of the universe, and I am uniquely and wonderfully made in the very image of God, and I am going to be one happy camper down on this earth!" Growing up, we did not let religion cause us to not like each other either. With a clear conscience, I sincerely believe that I can say there was a whole lot of unconditional love in Waycross when we were growing up; that is why I felt so compelled to author a book about the place of my upbringing. Yes, no place is perfect.

Every place has faults. All people have faults. Because of our sinful nature, we all make mistakes. None of us is perfect. And if you were to ever find a perfect place to live, as soon as you moved there, it would become imperfect! Let's enjoy life and enjoy sharing some great, fun stories! I cannot wait to read your stories one day!

I might add, you could have been in my shoes and lived in most every district of Waycross! The exciting part of that equation is that you would have ended up meeting amazing friends from all over the city! So many of them have remained friends after these almost sixty-five years!

The Rec Center

If you rode your bike down Riverside Drive from Alice Street, you would have to stop at the Riverside drugstore. The drugstore was a good stopping-off place for some candy and especially that new candy we all had discovered called rock candy. Remember those amazing crystal-looking pieces of candy? We thought, *Where did that kind of candy come from?*

Go up the hill, turn left, and at the bottom of the hill was the famous Rec Center. The early Saturday morning, basketball games were filled with parents, players, and fans from all over the city. Across the street, during baseball season, the Voigt fields were packed with people. I got my start in basketball right there in that metal gymnasium. The noise would bounce off those walls! I was a skinny kid, and my white basketball shorts made my legs look even skinnier. Later in life, I became a decent basketball player. But just starting out, it was a little rough. In one particular game, I remember my coach put me in, and I either stole the ball as a guard, or someone passed it to me. I got so excited. I think I reacted like Barney Fife would have. I took off down the court and shot two for points! Everybody was yelling, "Go, go, go," and I was going as fast as I could go. The problem was, they were saying, "Go, go, go the *other way*!" I had shot two points for the other team! I never really understood why after that game, my coach let me sit on the bench, for it seemed like a long time. Ya think?

The Rec Center hosted the well-known water shows of Waycross. To this date, I have not seen a water show quite like those. I remember a diver named Tom who set a record one night as I was watching. He did four over-and-over flips from the diving board until he hit the water. It was incredible! After that event, I invited my oldest sister, Bobbie Jean, to come and watch this guy. She did, and unbelievably, she ended up marrying him! They ended up having four children, but I don't think any of them became divers! Oh, this episode happened when we lived on Grove Avenue, which was straight up the hill and across Riverside Drive.

Across the street was a great park to swing, have picnics, run, play, and then get up your courage to cross the canal. There was a black canal pipe that was famous; no doubt, hundreds of kids have either walked or scooted on that pipe over the canal. Then there was that footbridge from the Rec Center to the huge ball fields.

One of biggest events for kids was baseball season. Teams from all over would meet on those fields and play citywide, and I even think statewide championships. I did not play on a team, but I sure did go and watch the games, for I had many friends who played. It was in this Little League Baseball Program that many skillful players went on to play high school and college baseball. If you ever get a chance to visit Waycross again, go by and see the old Rec Center, and it might just bring back many great memories!

Now that we have had a little intermission with some great episodes about other neighborhoods, the other side of the tracks, and the Rec Center, please allow me to drive you across town again. This time, my dad moved us, for sure, because of his job. He leased a building on Reynolds Avenue with a desire to open Bullard Supermarket. I don't know this for sure, but it is possible that Mr. Harris and my dad agreed this would be a good move; and if for some reason it did not play out to be successful, then Dad would go back to Harris Market. I know this: He loved the grocery business and his customers. So many things in life I learned from watching my dad work with people in the grocery store. We packed up and moved across town to Sweat Street. This house was right behind the grocery store.

Sweat Street

Nineteen sixty-four was the year we moved to Sweat Street for another adventure of living in Waycross. As I just mentioned, the reason was a good one. My dad and mom had started their own grocery store, and they called it Bullard supermarket. I can remember how excited we all were, having a grocery store named after our family. That was amazing to me as a young man. Dad had worked hard for years, helping manage other stores; and he decided to try having his own store. Across from the store was Settles' Pharmacy; it was great being able to know the Settle family. Great people! It is kind of ironic now looking back, but we lived on Sweat Street, and our entire family put much sweat in that grocery store!

Bullard Supermarket was a neat store. Dad was the owner and manager. Mom was the cashier. Ronnie was working in the meat market. Connie helped in any area that was needed. I think more in the office area. And Larry (that's me) worked in the produce and bagged groceries. It was there that I learned firsthand how hard the grocery business really was—so much work stocking shelves, keeping a store clean and well-groomed, pleasing the customer, and so many other areas of customer service. I'll never forget those words: "Larry, if you will bag the groceries the right way and be as kind as you can be, you might get a good tip." He was right. And I really appreciated our customers for "tipping"! The one uncomfortable memory of our store was I think that this was one of the stores where my dad was robbed at gunpoint. Bless him!

To give this idea about a store a chance, Dad had leased, rather than purchased, the building. But after a few years, he was invited back to work at Harris Market, and he decided to go. Unfortunately, Bullard Supermarket closed. Now we all were thinking, *Okay, what is next as far as "where will we live"?* By this time, I was in the seventh grade, still attending Quarterman Street School. I am grateful my parents worked out the details for me to remain in the same school district. Seventh grade was not particularly bad, for I looked forward to those square-dance classes we had! Remember that one girl in the neighborhood I mentioned earlier in our clubhouse days? Well, she was in that seventh-grade square-dance class! She was in school with us the whole time, but now that we were a little older, she seemed to be much more beautiful. The only thing I did not like were the frames she wore on her glasses: They were a little weird looking, like cat's-eyes! But really, that was quite all right because she was sweet and beautiful. Again, there was some small fighting moments over who would get to square dance with her. I have not seen her after all these years; I hope she grew up to have a great life. I really hope that is the case for all those cherished early childhood friends and class-mates at Quarterman Street School.

One thing for sure, in our family, *flexibility* was a trait we were all learning! Some people never learn that trait and go through their lives living with anger and bitterness because they haven't had things go their way. By the time I was in the seventh grade, I should have made up a button and worn it that said, "Just Be Flexible." So in a few moments, I will tell you about our moving across town to Magnolia Street. This time was a little different, for we, indeed, moved across the tracks!

Here is a good place to inject a few unique experiences that came my way. I am so thankful that my dad taught me to work and to be able to earn some spending money for myself. He worked hard, so why shouldn't we do the same?

Boiled Peanuts—Ten Cents a Bag

Let's go back just a little bit in our chronology. Remember the house on Grove Avenue? It was in that house as a fifth grader that I started my very first business. Dad would buy raw peanuts from the grocery store when fresh peanuts arrived. He taught me to soak them, salt them, and boil them. He helped me start a boiled peanut business, and it was really a wonderful experience.

After they were boiled, we would bag them up in those small bags that we would fill with candy at a store. The Waycross Tobacco Warehouse was just down the street on the corner of Riverside and Plant Avenues. During the season on Saturday, when the salespeople would come to town, and the farmers would sell their tobacco, the warehouse was a buzzing, busy place. I made up a container using a cardboard box lid, poked holes in the sides, ran some thick string through the holes, and tied a knot to put around my neck. Off I would go every Saturday for two summers in my fifth grade and into my sixth grade. I would make enough money on Saturday to pay my dad back for the raw peanuts, salt, and bags. The money I made for profit I put in a cigar box and hid it under the bed or in the closet. It was my very first business, and it was incredible what that little business did for me even later in my teenage years. I will go ahead and tell you some of it now. When I got through selling peanuts at the Tobacco Warehouse, if I had some left, I would put the box lid in my bicycle basket and ride downtown. I was excited about peanuts (they were so good), so I decided to go in each store downtown and try to sell them to the merchant owners. I will shorten this episode simply to say that when I went in Rivenbark's men's shop, I met the nicest man. His name was Hubert Rivenbark, and he would always buy some peanuts from me; that always made my day! That little peanut business helped me create valuable relationships with many store owners in downtown Waycross and later provided a rewarding opportunity for employment.

Things I Learned from My Dad in the Grocery Business

1. Treat every customer the same. Do your best, and you may get a good tip.
2. Open doors for the ladies after you put the groceries in the back seat of their car. Be a gentleman.
3. Bag the cold items together. Then in a separate bag, put all the dry items together; the customer will appreciate it.
4. Always put the container of eggs on the top of the cool item bag if there is room; otherwise put them in a separate little bag.
5. Always put the loaf of bread on the top of the dry item bad; otherwise put it in a separate bag.

Things I Learned from My Mama in the Restaurant Business

1. Welcome the customer with a friendly smile. Take them to their table. Never point them to their table.
2. When the customer's coffee cup is half empty, offer to fill it up without them having to ask.
3. Always be respectful and loyal to your boss.
4. Treat the customer with great service, and you will be surprised how well they will tip.
5. Even if you must walk to work, your boss needs you to be there. Don't complain.

Magnolia Street

Because Dad decided he was better at helping manage a store owned by someone else, he returned to work at Harris Supermarket. So of course, a new move was now in order. And where was it located? Across town! Yep, all the way over to Cherokee Heights on Magnolia Street.

As kids, we were unaware of the dynamics of growing up. As I've mentioned, it got a little confusing moving from one place to the next; but there was nothing we could do except go along and enjoy the ride. Yes, I must admit, it got somewhat embarrassing at times, especially when I would consider my friends who continued to live in the same houses throughout almost all of their childhood.

Magnolia was a good street and a good neighborhood to meet new friends at the end of my seventh grade and into the eighth. Our house on Magnolia was located directly across from Williams Heights Elementary School and was great for many reasons. One reason in particular was that it was close to the events held at the Waycross Memorial Stadium! We said we have moved way across the city. The wonderful thing was that we could walk to the football games, listen to concerts on our front porch, and be a little closer to our future high school. I remember the "Gospel Sings," the Hullabaloo concert, Gary Lewis, and it seemed like the lights were on quite often at the stadium. The football games were exciting for sure, and when the band played at halftime, it was thrilling. My oldest sister had been a majorette, and many times we got to see her march up and down the field with that marching band playing great football game music!

One thing that seemed to stay in my mind was the night they had an *All-Night Gospel Sing* at the memorial stadium. We lived right there, across the street. It was loud, and the place was packed; cars were everywhere. I remember sitting on the front porch listening to gospel music and hearing songs that were all about Jesus, heaven, family, love, America, military, patriotism, and friends—but mostly, songs that talked about the cross. After all, I lived in Way*cross*! I think it was during those kinds of moments that God was really working on my heart and speaking to me. Sadly, in my hard-hearted state as a young teenager, I would push those thoughts back. I really did not want to hear about Jesus. I really did not want to hear those kinds of things yet. Do you remember having those same thoughts as a teenager?

The only problem I could see about living on Magnolia was that the junior high I would be attending was a long way back across town on Mary Street. Wait a minute; that was where I lived when we first moved to Waycross! Remember the eighth-grade building on Mary Street, the old vocational building? How did that happen with the educational system? It was like, why? I think, no one ever explained it to us. It was just the way it was. So off to school I would go, riding my bike across town. It was fine, except when it rained, and I had to wear that yellow raincoat.

I would do all kinds of odd jobs like mowing grass, raking leaves and straw, just anything possible to make some extra money so I could begin buying my teenage clothes. After all, the styles were coming in, and I did not want to be left out. When I would make some clothing money, I would head down to Jake & Ed's, the Prim Shop, or Rivenbark's. While only an eighth grader, I had, for some reason, a craving for nice clothes. My dad always put his shirts in the cleaners to get them starched. Many of my friends seemed to like stylish clothes, so that gave me a desire to have sharp-looking ones as well.

On one occasion, I went to Jake & Ed's to see the newest style of pants, and I am rather sure that I bought the smallest waist size available. They allowed me to put a pair of multicolored (almost like a madras print) pair of pants on layaway for a few weeks. When I finally paid them off, I could not wait to wear them to school. I put them on, had a nice matching shirt, got on my bike, and rode from Magnolia Drive to the eighth-grade building on Mary Street. As soon as I walked in the classroom, my teacher met me. I think it was Mrs. Hargraves.

She said, "Larry, what do you have on?"

I said, "My new pair of pants!"

"Well, Larry, you cannot wear those at school. They are just too loud."

I had to ride my bike all the way across town and change my pants. That was somewhat embarrassing. But even worse, it was *so* far to go just to change a pair of pants! I am not sure why, but I seemed to always like adventure and experiencing something new. I am sure I was not alone, but in my mind, it seemed to be magnified. Ironically, soon after that episode, many teenage boys bought those Madras-style pants, and they became acceptable at school! Go figure!

Magnolia Street was a wonderful place to live. Many new friends and experiences in life took place in that new neighborhood. I think this was where I noticed a little more rebellion taking root in friends, and I probably should have not hung around some of them. But then again, who was I to ever judge anybody?

I remember sitting on the front porch one day when I heard the news that my mom's dad (Granddaddy) had "died and gone to heaven." I am thankful that Dad would make sure we got up and went to church on Sunday with him at Central Baptist Church, which was located close to Wilbur James Tire and the old YMCA. By the way, the YMCA was a great place to go shoot pool on Saturday. It was packed with young people!

I appreciate your going along with me today to see these houses we lived in; and in just a few moments, we will go across town again to Butler Street. Now that I was going into the ninth grade, and of course, my brother and sister were ahead of me a few years, this next house gave us many teenage memories!

Central Baptist Church

Many of my friends attended the Central Baptist Church on Brunel Street. I can remember going to Sunday school class and then to the morning worship service. A few of us always liked to sit in the balcony—first row—overlooking the crowd. One specific friend and I would always plan for the day by bringing a few straws and paper to make some good spitballs. Sad to say, during the service, we would go into war mode, aim at the necks of our friends sitting on the bottom floor, and shoot those crazy spitballs from the balcony; and on occasion, we would miss and hit the person next to them— not good! I think the preacher got wind about it, and soon we were stopped from that lawless behavior. I am sure we had to make some apologies to some older people who were hit by mistake! Thank you, preacher, for stepping in and being a great leader. As I look back, the terrible behavior I just described may just be the reason that pastor came by our house to visit me one day (when I hid underneath the kitchen table). I was a churchgoer but not a Christian. I did not know Jesus as my personal Savior until 1973. I am so grateful God has mercy on all of us Aren't you?

Things I Started to Realize regarding My Many Moves

- It finally hit me that we had moved to *so* many places in my early years.
- Because of a lack of understanding for all the moves, I could have been tempted to become somewhat bitter; I am pretty sure that I did not.
- I could have felt rejected, but for some reason, I saw my base of friends expanded.
- While some of the houses themselves did cause me embarrassment, I learned to not stay there in my thinking. I did not have a choice in the matter, and my folks were doing their best.
- For the most part, because I enjoyed meeting new people, the moves did not bother me.
- I was glad I had a mom and dad that worked hard, supported us, and provided a roof over our head. In fact, we had many roofs over our heads!
- By the time I was in the eighth grade, we had already moved eight times within the Waycross city limits.

Butler Street

Ninth grade was here, and I was now a high school student! You may be getting a bit frustrated reading about all these moves. Imagine having to do it. Teenagers usually become more conscious of their surroundings and of what their friends think about "this and that." It is a natural result of maturity. I wish I had known about that song that later became famous, "On the Road Again," for that was how we were feeling in the Bullard home. We had to be careful about having friends spend the night with us, for the next day their parents might have to pick them up from a different house. Just kidding of course! I do think from, time to time, it was asked of me, "Why do y'all move so much?" Truthfully, I had no understandable answer.

Butler Street was the place to be! We were around the corner from our old house on Alice Street and just down the street two blocks from where we had lived on Grove Avenue; so we were really close to so many fun places that had created memories just a few years ago. That was cool!

Another season of life had begun: attending Waycross High School on Ava Street. Guess where Ava Street was located? Are you ready for this? Just one block from where we just moved from on Magnolia Street. Dear readers and friends, I promise you, all of this is true and authentic.

My sweet sister was three years ahead of me in school; so when we moved, it was her senior year of high school. The year was 1967. Unfortunately, my brother had gone through some tough times a couple of years earlier in the tenth grade. Sadly, a teacher embarrassed him and made fun of him in class. He was told to go to the principal's office. But instead, he left, went home, and never returned to school. I just remember my dad and mom had to go to the school to validate what had happened; and it was verified. Of course, like all difficulties in life, we must forgive and press on. My brother went on to work odd jobs until he was old enough to join the navy. I'll never forget the day he "shipped out to Guam after completing his basic training at Great Lakes, Illinois. He told me years later that he forgave that teacher in his heart. Today, if a teacher talked to students and said some of the things that were said back then, that teacher would be fired. For certain, no student should be embarrassed in class by some-one in authority just because they are not perceived to be as good compared to others. Never should that behavior be tolerated within our American school system!

I wish there had been reconciliation at the time between Ronnie and his teacher. It is tough carrying those kinds of things in your heart. Let me say this in passing, like in the movie *Frozen* and the great song "Let it Go," there are some things in our life journey that we just need to *let go*. Years later, it dawned on me that the same teacher also seemed to have it out for me; but I think, because she had realized her mistake and did not want to repeat it, she was nicer and kinder to me. I know you are thinking, *What was it that she said to Ronnie?* Her statement was that one day my brother would grow up and be "just like our dad." She had known our dad in the grocery business, knew that we had moved around a lot and that we really did not have very much; she had used her knowledge to be judgmental, unkind, and to create pain.

In life, everyone makes mistakes, and we have all said and done things that brought shame in some fashion. Forgiveness is a virtue, and if others have hurt you, wounded you, and caused you pain, do your best to receive grace to forgive and let it go! The older we get, the sweeter life should be. Get better and not bitter!

Butler Street in 1967 was where I experienced my brother's 1956 red four-door Chevrolet with the gearshift on the floor. What a great ride! While working and selling clothes in a downtown ladies' shop, my sister had bought a car as well. It was a beautiful light green 1963 VW Bug, and she loved it! Connie's close friends, Marcia and Rosemary, and so many others, would come over and spend the night. They would have so much fun, playing the 45 rpm records on her baby blue hi-fi stereo then slip over to Dairy Queen in the Bug!

Dad had also recently bought a new car. Well, it was new to us, but it really was a 1962 Buick Electra, and it was electric through and through. It was the greatest car to drive! If you turned on the radio to Big Jeff and other local stations, and you could hear some great teenage music back in the day! It was starting to be fun as a teenager, experiencing all these cool things. The day came for me to get my learner's permit from the Georgia State Patrol Office out on Memorial Drive. It was happening; I could drive! The best part: Our permits allowed us to drive by ourselves until it got dark.

Having a day date with your girlfriend was cool; we just had to be home before dark. One problem we always seemed to have was that of leaving the car radio on our favorite channel. Dad would keep telling me not to listen to "that kind" of music. It was beach music and, yes, a little bit of rock. When the day came to get the permanent driver's license, we could then drive after dark. At that point, we really felt grown up. It was like "the light just turned on" in another phase of life!

Butler Street had so many memories! The night I woke up, and the house next door was on fire. It really startled me, not just for the moment but also in life. I just remember my entire room lit up as red as fire, and for a moment, I thought I had died and fallen into that place called hell. It was so real and shook me for some time. I had heard about a place called hell in Sunday school and church when I was younger, but I had begun to drift away from going to church. That fire next door did get my attention about the brevity of life; but I soon pushed away those thoughts by filling my mind with other things.

In a house of three teenagers, the long phone cord that ran from the dining room into the living room and even into the bedroom was the center of attention. We could close the door and talk to our friends, and if we had a girlfriend, it gave us a little privacy. Looking back, I realize that kids should not need to hide behind a door to talk to their girlfriend, should they?

Butler Street was a much larger house than we had been used to living in, and I can remember that having the extra space was like a breath of fresh air. My close friends lived just down the street. We did not get together as we had in our elementary years, but it was still always good to see them. Life has a way of changing relationships, but that is a natural thing. Now that I was in high school, my list of friends was expanding. Wow, we were finally growing up!

Waycross High School

S ports, cars, music, girlfriends, work, and so many areas of life were instrumental to change our thinking as we were progressing toward adulthood. The truth was, now we were now closer to adulthood than to childhood. It was the last year for Waycross High to be located on Ava Street. The new classrooms were beautiful, modern, and filled with energy and dreams for all of us! The new gymnasium would be the place for our exciting basketball games. The new track behind the school would be the place for some exciting track-and-field events. One problem I had was that I had to go to work every day after school; well, it was not a problem, but it did prevent me from getting involved in sports like I wished. Back then, just like today, you just had to do what you had to do!

I did get to join the cross-country team in high school, and that was a great outlet for emotions and even frustrations! Our coach would take us out Central Avenue in a good way, drop us all off, and we would run back to the school. That run was a great time to ponder my problems and try to create solutions. However, after some time, the run kept getting longer because Coach kept lengthening the drop-off point! I was an okay runner, but we had some faster runners who went on to do great things in our State Cross Country Championship.

We had some of the most fantastic football games at Waycross Memorial Stadium, which is now called the Swamp for the Ware County Gators. I remember, we would fill up the bleachers with cowbells, cheering and yelling, "We got spirit, yes we do. We got spirit, how about you?" I remember our fighting Waycross Bulldogs!

We had so many great friends at Waycross High School and at Ware County High School! So I would like to also dedicate this writing to my high school friends who affected my life in some way, either with a good word or a good action; and I say, thank you, Danny, Marion, Troy, Tony, R. L., Wade, Doug, Bonnie, Elaine, Lynda, Janie, Peggy, Becky, Sam, Doran, Sammie, Connie, Anne, Carol, Patty, John, Stan, Herbie, Joann, Larry, Ric, Harold, Gene, Jack, Harold, Lewis, Kenny, Alex, Bud, Chip, Louise, Raymond, Rosemary, Teresa, Shirley, Lealane, Dave, Harvey, Becky, Donald, Johnny, Lionel, Jimmy, Sandra, Terry, Kermit, Wylene, Geraldine, Sandra, Eugene, Jimmy, Rosemary, Kenny, Janet, Kelly, Janet, Leta, Andy, Glenda, Penny, Susan, Vicki, Lois, Kenny, Cathy, James, Norma, Robert, Tom. Tina, Theodore, Amaras, Kenny, Harold, Wanda, Linda, Teresa, Ronnie, Bertha, Patricia, Zeda, Linda, Ronnie, Larry, Paul, Karen, Virginia, Janet, Andrea, Meatreall, Freddie, Rosemary, Phyllis, Paula, Kathy, Janelle, Larry, Clarence, Randy, Winky, Ronnie, Maureen, Bruce, Patricia, Robert Hamp, Sharon, Ricky, Lawanna, Nancy, Hannah, Eddie, Diane, Linda, Jimmy, Gloria, Debra, Gwen, Jimmy, Caroline, Debbie, Deborah, Kay, Jackie, Ricky, Janice, Theonoplis, Jackie, Lovel, Lamar, Dennie, Janis, Debra, Patricia, Charlotte, Walter, Michael, Stella, Dianne, Linda, Harriett, Lee, Marsha, Delores, Pat, Marvin, Rusty, Ronald,

Tank, Heather, Greg, Becky, Katie, Brenda, Sharon, Louise, Molly, Patsy, Roseann, Alvin, Mary, Danna, Doyle, Debra, Vickie, Melissa, Edwin, Tommy, Emory, Donald, Janice, Billie, Larry, Bill, Gloria, Steve, Peggy, Janelee, Mike, Pat, Ronald, Cleveland, Sharon, Carolyn, James, Linda, Gloria, Beth, Althea, Sandra, Dale, Larry, Jake, Chip, Steve, Jean, Kathy, Kenneth, Judy, James, Cassie, Havis, Pamela, Renee, Glenda, Dwayne, Deborah, Wayne, Kathy, Janice, Patricia, Carl, Mopsy, Larry, Sharon, Billy, Melody, David, Shan, Linda, Dorothy, Gail, Ronald, Ann, Brenda, Robert, Cora, Kathy, Ann, Yvonne, Wylder, Jimmy, Debbie, Tamara, Curran, Neal, Bill, Berniel, Johnny, Ralph, Hazel, Ronnie, Randy, Elgin, Mazie, Ruth, Larry, Buster, Martha, Caroline, Julia, Freddie, Cleveland, Cleve, Harper, Wanda, Gary, Lawrence, Melvene, Edward, Avis, Dianne, Stephen, Mary, Brenda, Debra, Jackie, Edna, Carol, Joseph, David, Kay. Forgive me if I did not spell each name correctly.

After I listed these names of my classmates, I took a few minutes to pray for each one and their families. Some have already entered heaven and are walking on the streets of gold! May their families be in good health, and may their core values be passed down upon the next generation!

May I say *thank you*, dear friends, in grade school, middle, and high school! We got to cross paths in this life's journey, and it was a great privilege to see you in the hallways, classes, or in other settings! Thank you, and God bless each of you!

Things I Learned from Many of My Teachers

1. Listen in class, and you will not have to study as hard.
2. Do your homework, or you will fail. (You think?)
3. Do your best to not be late for class.
4. Practice kindness with your classmates.
5. Take good notes in class.

Great Ride to High School from a Great Friend

O ne friend was Ricky. He had a new 1969 Super Beetle with that wind scoop on the back; it was one beautiful car. Ricky and I had become good friends. Every day, he drove all the way across town from Cherokee Heights to pick me up on Butler Street. I look back over it and realize, more than ever, what a long way it was to go to pick up a friend for school. Those were some fantastic days! If ever someone showed me how to be a friend, it was Ricky. Years have passed, and we are still good friends!

I love to get together with friends after all these years and share stories. Recently, another great friend, Jack, reminded me about one of our crazy, lawless days. As wacky as it was, it brought much laughter to our souls! Jack loves to tell the story; ask him, and he can tell you his version! When we take time for one another, it is amazing what our friends can help us remember; and some have more detailed memories than mine for sure. By the way, if you ever get a chance to be in Waycross, go by his store and say hello to Jack Lott; he will give you great customer service! The last time we were together at a Waycross High reunion, he reminded me of stories I had forgotten, and we spent much time laughing about those crazy high school days!

Here is some incredible news for my readers: Butler Street, 1967–1970, was the last house we lived in during my high school years. But soon afterward, we moved to Jane Street on the other side of town!

Girlfriend or "Girlfriend"

I think I am remembering accurately that during our elementary days at school, the boys and girls would just somehow find each other in a classroom, hallway, playground, or a neighborhood. Those were the first days of young connections, and it was sweet, innocent, and much fun. It was always great saying you had a girlfriend. I guess we should really spell it like this—girl friend—because they were girls, and they were friends. Now in some situations, one may have become a girlfriend; but most of the time, it was a boy and a girl just being great friends.

I have a profound respect for those girls that were my girlfriend or my "girlfriend"! It was fun getting to know their parents, going to their houses, laughing, having fun, going to movies, enjoying swimming, Halloween parties, dances, the beach, and sometimes, attending a family reunion with them. Now that I look back over those days, one big event was missing in my life: going to a youth event at a church. The closest I got to that was going to YMCA camp for a few summers.

I remember in those elementary grades the little sparks that would fly concerning some sweet, pretty girl, and I could not wait to see her in class. Then I remember those middle school and high school years when the feelings were more cherished, and the conversations lasted a little longer. I look back and am thankful for those sweet, precious girls. Each of us was making choices in life! Going to a movie, taking a bike ride, going out to eat, taking a ride in the car with each other's parents, attending the Friday or Saturday night dances in the American Legion building—all were a part of the growing-up process. We enjoyed going to basketball or football games, cheering on those mighty Waycross Bulldogs, and, yes, going

76

to our junior-senior proms. Remember having our moms help us order a corsage to give our date for the prom? I sincerely hope I was a gentleman and showed enthusiastic respect and honor to those who were a onetime date, a long-term girlfriend, or a fun playmate on the playground during recess.

Rivenbark's Men's and Ladies' Shop

One of the highlights of growing up in Waycross was my time spent working with Mr. Hubert and Mr. Bill at Rivenbark's men's and ladies' shop. It was an honor working with so many other shop employees, including Kirk, Bill, Bob, and a host of part-time men and ladies. When I was twelve years of age, this was the merchant that loved to buy boiled peanuts from me when I would bring them downtown. When I was seventeen, I went down and applied for a job. I really loved clothes and wanted to work at this exclusive clothing store. To my surprise, Mr. Hubert hired me, and soon my journey in the clothing industry began.

Mr. Bill, the granddad, seemed to take a likin' to me and began the training process with me. He took time to teach me how they greeted the customer and how to size up a gentleman with the right suit or sports coat size. Mr. Bill really knew the industry well. He would say, "When you do not have a customer, take time to match up about five shirts and five ties with each suit so that when you are asked to help find a match, you would be ahead of the game." Brilliant idea! Good advice, Mr. Bill!

Mr. Hubert introduced me to their clients and made me feel very welcome, almost like another family member. In some ways, he really did treat me like another son; he was so very kind and went out of his way to make me feel included. He seemed to know everybody. I soon realized that, having lived in so many areas of the city, I now had the opportunity to invite those many high school friends to come shop at Rivenbark's. When a new Gant shirt would come in, I would call my friends. Do you remember how the girls liked the boys to wear the shirts with the loop on the back? They would take the loops off and keep them in their purses. I never really understood, but it was a girl thing! We sold Villager in the ladies' section, and on some Saturdays, it would be wall-to-wall, especially when the newest styles had just been displayed on the floor.

I am grateful that, as a young seventeen-year-old, I had the opportunity to work for such outstanding people. In 1972, when I moved to Milledgeville to attend Georgia College, Mr. Hubert made one phone call to Mr. Sammy Little at the Coventry shop in Milledgeville, and I had a job waiting for me when I arrived and was ready to start working. It was amazing to me how he interested he would be in my future!

The clothing interest stayed with me for many years. Later, while living in Indiana, I got a job at Carson, Pierre, and Scott department store selling men's clothing. I think it is enormously powerful how people can invest in your life and how that influence can stay with you for many years. May I say thank-you to the Rivenbark family for including me and giving me the opportunity to work in such an exceptional place! When you travel to downtown Waycross in these days, the only exclusive men's shop is Jake & Ed's, and Steve is still there, making a difference in the lives of people after all these years. I can remember when he played for the Bulldogs! Recently, I stopped by to say hello, and before I knew it, Steve had that measuring tape out around my neck, stomach, chest, arms, and ordered me a special light blue striped shirt. Thanks, Steve!

Things I Learned Working
at Rivenbark's

1. Shine your shoes, and you will perform better as a salesperson.
2. Put a little starch in your shirts; you will look more professional.
3. Dress nice, be neat, and always clip your fingernails.
4. Notice your customer; the details are important.
5. Use breath mints, gum, or whatever to keep your breath smelling good for the customers.

Jane Street

As I began to mature, I also began to realize that my dad did not make very much money. As most fathers would, he did his best to provide for us. My parents never owned a home until we made that last move to Jane Street in 1970. And, dear friend, that was exactly what happened after my high school graduation: Dad and Mom bought a home on Jane Street! When I ride by now, all I see is an empty lot with grass and the old driveway. This is the house where I could walk to work at Rivenbark's. Even after high school, I did not have my own vehicle, so I would continue to borrow my dad's car for dating, ball games, events, and just taking a drive on a Friday or Saturday night. This is the house we lived in when I decided to go off to Georgia College in Milledgeville. This is also the house where my parents lived when I was drafted, the last year of the Vietnam draft. Jane Street was the address where I brought my girlfriend home from college to meet my parents and family. Yes, Jane Street was the last of the many houses in which I had resided since my preschool years, which began on Mary Street. How far away was Mary Street? Just one block away! I had come full circle!

This life story I am sharing with you is about a family that moved ten times in twelve years! My mom and dad knew the Lord as their Savior. It was a great joy to stand at their celebration of life services years ago and honor our parents. God used them to teach me and my siblings many lessons in life. I also did not appreciate my parents as much as I should have until after they had left this earth. No doubt, this is true in many of our lives.

I do know that everything down here on earth is temporal. This world is not my home; we are just passing through. Our treasures are laid up beyond the blue. The Scriptures teach us that we are just strangers and pilgrims here, and that we will one day leave this earth for our eternal home. The only true, stable home any of us will possess will be when we get to heaven!

So I share my life story with a heart of gratitude for my parents, teachers, family, employers, and friends like you! I appreciate your taking time to allow me to share these writings with you! Perhaps along the way, someone will be encouraged in their life's journey by the simple stories shared by this friend and author of *Growing Up Where the Ways Crossed*!

Great Shopping
Downtown Waycross

Whether it was a larger store or a smaller shop, I can remember the thrill of a shopping experience as a kid and later as a teenager. JCPenney, Waycross Drugs, Fashion Shoppe, Friedman's Jewelry, Sims Jewelry, Churchwell's, Moody Jewelry, Scotty Drugs, Spears Drug, Kellam Pharmacy, Zachary Furniture, Herrin Furniture, Singleton Furniture, Walker Hood Furniture, Lott Furniture, Walker Hood Furniture, Dianna Shoppe, Gibson Furniture, Colonial Grocery, Bradshaw's, Lanier and Register, Barger's Bakery, Elliston's Drugstore, Commercial Bank, Southern Bank, First National Bank, Sears, Western Auto, Firestone, Goodyear, R. L. Walker Chevrolet, Prim Shop, Rivenbark's, Jake & Ed's, Yarbrough's, and Goodman's are only a few of the merchants that kept the good citizens of Waycross happy with their wares. I probably have left out some but not intentionally for sure. Waycross had some wonderful places to shop in those great days. The good news is that new businesses are coming back downtown—thanks to people who have stayed in Waycross through the years!

Remember the drugstores and their fountains with rotating seats? You could just twist round and round waiting on your hot dog with slaw or chili. How about a Cherry Coke or perhaps a Vanilla Coke? Want a great milkshake? There was nothing as good in a downtown shop or drugstore. If you ever wanted to know what was going on in Waycross, you could go sit on a swivel seat, place an order, and walk away with a little more information. Barbershops and beauty shops were fun places to go, not to just get a haircut or a wave but to find out what was happening in Waycross.

Connie worked at the Dianna Shoppe, and when I worked downtown, on occasion, we would meet at Spears Pharmacy to sit and enjoy lunch together. I think I remember even going to Barger's for a great cup of chili and oyster crackers! How many of us enjoyed shopping at Kress's or McCrory's? What great memories of Downtown Waycross! Some of the very best slaw or chili dogs were found in the pharmacies throughout the town! Absolutely delicious, especially when you could get a toasted bun!

Take a Stroll Downtown Now—I Believe It Is Coming Back

Take a walk downtown in 2021, and you can remember how it was back in the day. A tremendous group of people have worked hard to keep Waycross alive downtown. In the last year or so, many new businesses have opened, and that is exciting to see! Thank you for doing your best to continue to help develop the downtown area! Time goes by, the clock ticks, and we can never have what we once had; but it truly is exciting to see progress and a city begin to come alive again! It takes work, thought, diligence, and leadership to make it happen; so let's offer help and encouragement, not criticism and degrading verbiage. Together, we can all make a difference! We are so glad to know that the Ritz is now offering musical theater. And how would you like to hear the good news that the Lyric is reopening? Nothing is impossible! Nothing is impossible when there is a desire, the people, and diligence to move forward; but of course, that is the case with any endeavor!

The Ritz, The Lyric

Many a young man held his girlfriend's hand for the first time in one of those theaters downtown. Remember how it worked? I think there was an art to making it happen. So you and your date were sitting in the movie theater. You were scared to make that first move to hold her hand. But remember, she was probably thinking the same thing; she was scared also. You would pretend to cough, or you might cough; and when you covered your mouth with your elbow/arm, when you were done, the arm would go around the back seat of the chair. After all, you might need to put your arm around her to comfort her during the scary movie or the most intense moment of the movie. If you were not into the arm thing but really wanted to hold her hand, this was a bit tricky. You had to both share the arm rest and just go for it. You would move your hand close to her hand and just contact the pinky finger. If yours touched hers, and she did not move hers, then you were in good shape. If you got past that giant pinky sequence, then holding hands was a sweet moment with that person you really cared about.

we all have been through it, and all of us have been rejected at some point as well. It really is probably best to not even go there until you are married or at least until you think you are heading in that direction together! The best way I can describe the pinky-finger thing is like going fishing in a South Georgia pond, throwing out your fishing line with some good bait, and when the fish begins to nibble, you just give a little jerk; and hopefully it hooks the fish. Well, probably not a good analogy! All that is to say, good ole Ritz and Lyric Theatres!

City Auditorium

How can we forget? After all these years, just drive by, and you will remember those amazing events that took place at the City Auditorium with the Tams, Swingin' Medallions, Otis Redding, Percy Sledge, and so many old-time favorites. One momentous event my sister and I attended was the citywide dance contest. Chubby Checker's music had grabbed the nation's attention. Connie entered the limbo contest and won! I entered the twist contest, and believe this or not, I won also! I think she won a certificate to get a wave at some hair salon, and I won a leather belt! I think it was an authentic alligator belt. They were popular at school! How did we prepare for the contests? It was my sister's world-famous stereo that I mentioned earlier. Connie's friends would come over, dance to the music, and invite me into their dance group; so through their influence, I won the twist contest!

West Drive-In

Today, the original building (while under another name and occupied by another owner) is still located across from the Hog-N-Bone Restaurant on Memorial Drive. Troy, my good buddy, had some cousins whose family owned West Drive-In. Because of their goodness, we got jobs there as curb hops. We are talking about real *American Graffiti* stuff. Cherry Cokes, milkshakes, hamburgers, french fries, onion rings; you could pull up, sit in your car, and one of us would bring out your order. As curb hops, we did not deliver the food on roller skates, and I am glad. I never was a very good skater. Troy and others could tear up a skating rink, but I was missing something! Great memories at West Drive-In. Let me add this footnote: I have recently stopped by the bakery that is now located on the West Drive-In property. Their products are delicious! Check them out!

Tuffy's Drive-In

I never worked there, but many times did I sit there and order their celebrated foot-long hot dog! You had to drive a little way out of town to get there, but it was worth the drive. I think, looking back, it was one of the best kept secrets of Waycross. This was where you could go and meet the girls from Ware County High School. Many of the guys at Waycross High School did get a little upset because boys came all the way from Blackshear to visit Tuffy's! We found out later, it was because they wanted to meet the Ware County girls and perhaps enjoy a special order of french fries or a burger especially after a ball game! In other words, they would come to move in on our territory!

Kentucky Fried Chicken
Comes to Town

I am not sure how the news traveled so fast across the city when a new place was opening, but it did. There was no Google or Facebook, but the word got out rather quickly. One advantage of moving a lot, and living in so many different neighborhoods was the fact that my friends would call and let me know what was happening in other parts of town. The word came about KFC having a grand opening right off Memorial Drive. I made my way over on my bike, ready to enjoy some of the opening fanfare. I heard there were some giveaways, and I guess it did not bother me to sample some of that famous, tasty chicken either! Waycross was booming with many new businesses coming to town!

Today, the KFC does not exist in that location but has relocated on Plant Avenue going toward Blackshear. You may also be a fan of Maryland Fried Chicken! They have some good chicken as well, and their original store is still located in the same place on State Street.

Burger Chef in Waycross

I could spend much time writing about our experiences at the Burger Chef. Definitely, it was the "happening" place! Everybody knew everybody on Friday night after the ball games. The hamburgers and fries were delicious, but the enjoyment of friends was incredible! For sure, the one and only pay phone booth stayed busy all night as we lined up to wait our turn to make a call. The Burger Chef experience was probably the closest thing we had to the *American Graffiti* movie, with cars lined up, people playing their radio, and even some dancing, going on in the parking lot. Let me just say here that many memorable moments took place there, and most of it was simply good, laughing fun with friends in the parking lot! You go by that location now; it is an empty parking lot, but Jerry J's is right next door!

7-Eleven and Jerry J's
on Plant Avenue

Yes, Burger Chef was a booming place to hang out, especially after a ball game on Friday or Saturday night. Well, the word came that a 7-Eleven store was opening right next to the Burger Chef. I heard about it and took off to see what was happening! They were having a hot dog-eating contest, and you could win a prize. Naturally, I was right in the middle of that contest. Not only did I enter it, I won it! I think I was in the seventh grade or so. I managed to eat seven hot dogs on that exciting day at the grand opening. They gave us one drink to wash it all down. When it was all over, I was feeling rather sick. So up came the dogs on the hood on someone's car parked in front! It was terrible, but I just could not help it. They announced the winner, and to my surprise, I walked away with a six-pack of Coca-Cola, the grand prize! Imagine!

Years later, Jerry J's opened an excellent restaurant in that same location. If you are traveling through town, stop by and get an amazing sausage-egg biscuit. You will tell your friends! When I get the opportunity, I love to go to Jerry J's for breakfast for a couple of reasons. First of all, the food and customer service are excellent as they operate their business with great integrity and value the customer. Second, when I go, I either run into someone from years ago, or I see a sweet group of senior adults (like me!) eating, talking, and remembering the old days.

Soap Box Derby

Take a little drive down Plant Avenue, turn right onto Ava Street, go under the crossing; and at the first street, turn left. Head up the road, and there, right in front of the Jewish synagogue, was where, years ago, the Soap Box Derby was held. What seemed like a giant hill in our young eyes was little more than a steep incline. But how exciting was the preparation for and the participation in that iconic contest! Once, my dad helped me build a derby to enter the race! Mine was rather simple; it was made from either extraordinarily sturdy cardboard or plywood. We painted it, decorated it, and put some good wheels on for speed. We must have gone 100 mph; it seemed that way anyway. But it was probably more like 10 mph! I did not win that race, but it sure was fun being a part of the Soap Box Derby in Waycross!

First Skateboards in Waycross

B uy a pair of metal skates, take the wheels off, screw them to a thick piece of board about two feet long, and you were ready for skateboarding behind Memorial Hospital down Alice Street. We lived down the street, so the word traveled quickly to build a skateboard and meet at the parking lot behind the hospital about 6:00 p.m. after the employees went home from work. You are talking about fun; no wonder these kids today love skate boarding—it is a blast! We called it "skateboarding under the lights." We would have as many as ten to twenty skateboarders at one time. Little did we know back then that skateboarding would become a worldwide Olympic event, and you could become a world champion! Most of the kids that came were much better at it than I was, but it was a fun time together, complete with skinned-up knees, arms, hands, and some bruises as well. It would have been nice if I could have kept that first skateboard I owned.

Lagging on the Wall—Competition

Today it is cornhole or washer toss, but it was called lagging years ago. Remember, all you needed was good wall and some good concrete. If you had a nickel, penny, dime, or if you had saved up for a good day, you could lag for a quarter. The closest one to the wall was the winner!

If you happen to throw a leaner, it was hard to beat unless someone else hit yours and knocked it down. As a kid, spending some time on Saturday lagging was a good pastime. Not only that, but you might also just walk away with more money than you brought to play.

Downtown Miniature Race Car Track

I remember this place so well. Someone came into town with an idea to start a miniature stock car racetrack and built it on the inside of one of the empty stores. That was one fantastic idea! It also was a little bit expensive, either you could rent the eight-inch race cars for $3.00–$5.00 an hour, or you could buy your own and bring it in a fancy wooden case. I think Saturday was the busy time, and the races would pull people in from different cities as far away as Valdosta, Fitzgerald, or Jesup. You literally felt like you were going to a miniature Daytona Firecracker 400. I think some of the car owners put numbers on their cars in honor of their favorite stock car driver. It was fun while it lasted. I think that idea died out after a couple of years, but it was fun!

Laura S. Walker State Park

Let's go back in our minds to the occasional weekends at Laura S. Walker. The pool was gigantic, and the crowds came from everywhere. Back in the day, families would bring their ski boats, and some of the best skiing around was found on that lake. It seemed like it was a big lake; but then again, that may have been our childhood perspective. You could smell food everywhere with charcoal grills all fired up, cooking chicken, steaks, hot dogs, and hamburgers. Many families would rent a full-size pavilion and have an old-fashion family reunion! I guarantee you, per capita, there were more watermelons at the lake on a weekend than any other place in Georgia. Well, we thought that anyway. By the way, while we are talking about watermelons, let us not forget the famous yellow-meat type melon. When you saw one of those, it was special! All you needed was a good washrag, paper towels, a box of Morton salt, a knife, and soon the watermelon juice would be down to your elbows on a sweltering summer day! So good!

There was something also incredibly special about Laura S. Walker: It was that famous jukebox that lit up the wooden floor for Saturday and even Sunday afternoon dancing. I know you were not supposed to dance on Sunday, but for some reason, they did at the lake. For newcomers, just go out Brunswick Highway about nine miles and turn right. If you visit the lake these days, the pool is gone, but the old building where the jukebox was is there, and the pavilions are there. No longer will you find skiing on the lake. Just like everything, in time, it all seems to change. Life is that way for all of us!

DK's BBQ

DK's, after over fifty years of service, has a BBQ sandwich with homemade sauces that is amazing, delicious, and mouthwatering! I recently stopped in and left with a bag of the junior and regular size, smashed-down sandwiches, which are their trademark. We were going to take them, sit down, and enjoy an evening, but we ended up eating them before we got out of the parking lot! I shared with the owners that we wanted to include DK's in the book, and they were well pleased. Everybody knows about DK's in Waycross. You are talking about good, hardworking, friendly people, still continuing their legacy, making the famous DK sandwich! Congratulations to their family for staying open all these years and making hundreds and thousands of people happy with their food and service! Also, thank you for your excellent customer service to your patrons!

Dad's Grocery

I really am not sure why the store was called Dad's, but it sure felt like you were at home when you opened the screen door and walked inside. If you remember, it was on Plant Avenue. The old concrete floor, counters, cash register, and most of all, the candy counter! What was your favorite candy? Remember the candy cigarettes? How about at Halloween—the yellow wax whistles, large wax lips, little juice-filled wax cola cartons, and chocolate milk in that little container with the tab that you could tear off and collect? If you had time to buy them before you got to school in the morning, you could get a few Mary Janes filled with peanut butter. I now know the reason I was so hyper in school!

We all remember that tragic day when the huge flood came and washed Dad's Grocery into the canal! That was a sad day, for we never had that wonderful place to visit ever again.

Clay Pits

I recall many times as a young man going to the clay pits with a bunch of guys and swimming where the water was clear, and the bottom was white sand. Most of us had to go on Sunday afternoon because of sports programs or work during the week. That is the first time I ever heard the word skinny-dipping. I guess it was the thing to do, and we just jumped in, swam like fish, and wore our dry clothes home. You think our parents might have done the same thing? I guess we will never know! I do remember the scary part of that bike ride home, especially when the sun was going down. That old cemetery was at the entrance, and we had to ride our bikes past it to and from the clay pits. I really was not fond of that part of the adventure!

Spook Light

How can we remember Waycross and forget to mention the spook light? I think, in most cases, it was simply a good excuse to drive out after dark with your girlfriend. When we got there, cars were everywhere. We all had the same idea: to see that spook light. I really am glad none of us was alone. We would all sit in our cars, waiting on the light, about a quarter of a mile away, to appear in the middle of the railroad tracks. I don't think anybody had the nerve to walk close enough to it to find out exactly what it was, but tales have it that someone fell off a train caboose and was killed on the tracks in that spot. I am sure there were many tales of the spook light. If you ever find out exactly what it was, let some of us know! It has been a mystery all these years!

The Bonnie and Clyde Movie Came to Waycross

(I relay this incident to offer a word of wisdom for young people not to mirror any wrong behavior after they have viewed any movie filled with violence or lawlessness.)

I will be as discreet as possible in telling this story, but I can tell you that the 1967 *Bonnie and Clyde* movie had a significant impact on many of our minds and, consequently, our behaviors! This tenth-grade episode begins with a good friend (I will withhold his name in deference to his privacy) and me going to see the movie on a Saturday afternoon. My memory says we drove his mother's white Comet. My friend had gotten in the habit of squealing the tires, burning rubber, and then gunning it. That Comet was one fast car for sure! So off to the movie we went to see bank robbers, thieves, shootings, and mayhem. We really did not know what to expect from the movie; all we knew was that it was packed in the theater!

Those of you that saw it, remember that it left you hanging on the edge of your seat. The movie was over! What are we going to do now? It is not late yet. We headed to his house to check in with the parents, parked the car, and walked down to the Fred Voigt baseball field. We loved to roam, and after seeing this movie, it put a roaming spirit inside of us. We walked up to the concession booth, which, of course by now, was closed with no one around—idea! Back to the house, we ran, opened up the car trunk, and out came the crowbar!

Here we go; my good friend and I backed down to the concession booth. Did you notice, I did not say "confession booth" but concession, where the goodies are, like Cokes, baseballs, candy, chips, and more Cokes and more baseballs.

The dark had settled in, and we found ourselves living out some of what we had just seen in the movie theater. Yes, we broke in, stole baseballs and drinks, then took off running. We took the bottled drinks down to the canal and broke them on the concrete walls just to hear them explode. The baseballs—well we had many buddies, so we kept them and gave them out Monday at school to our friends! Again, how stupid and lawless can two teenagers get!

At 2:00 p.m. that same day—I will never forget what happened—over the intercom system on the way to gym class came the announcement: "Will Larry Bullard and —! —please come to the principal's office." We passed each other going into the gym, and we *knew* that *they* knew. But how? Here's how: That morning in homeroom class, I wrote another friend a note to tell him how great the movie had been and all the fun we'd had over the weekend and how we wished he'd been with us! The bell rang, and he accidentally left the note on the desk. Boy, was I stupid! I had *signed the note*, "Your friend, Larry!" Being called into the principal's office was not only scary but extremely embarrassing! In honesty, our weekend activity had not been normal behavior for us. We truly had been under the villainous influence of Bonnie and Clyde. No, actually, we had been under the influence of our sinful nature, which tends to think, believe, and then behave in wrong and lawless ways. It takes character to do the right thing. I must admit, on that Saturday, before Monday, neither one of us had had enough character to say "no" to the temptation to do wrong.

Off to the office we went, and awaiting us was a policeman. He took us in the car to the police station downtown; and one of the hardest phone calls we ever made was to our parents, confessing to them what we had done. We were extremely sorry and embarrassed, and it was indeed painful knowing that we had hurt our parents, ourselves, and had brought shame on our names at school. Thanks, Bonnie and Clyde, for your influence—not! Our punishment was community service and fervent promises that we would never behave that way again.

How many of you reading this remember similar episodes in your life? Those kinds of memories are not fun to even talk about;

but perhaps, some young person reading this will have enough character not to follow suit with what they just read in our story! I am glad to report that this story does have a good ending.

Years later, both my good friend and I asked Jesus to be our Savior! Upon our confession of faith, all our sins, mistakes, and wrongdoings were covered by what the Bible says is the blood of Jesus Christ! That was the greatest day of our lives! To be forgiven is such a wonderful thing! One of my favorite Scripture verses is found in Psalm 25:7 and starts out with the powerful words, "Remember not the sins of my youth, nor my transgressions: according to thy mercy remember thou me for Thy goodness' sake, O Lord."

Waycross Fairgrounds

I think everybody around this region looked forward to the annual Waycross-Ware County Fair. It was located at Memorial Drive, and it is still there today. I loved the days when we could get discounted tickets; I think they gave them out at school. As a child, we rode all those kids' rides. But when we became teenagers, we hit the big ones like the Bullet. As you sat in that enclosed cage, the Bullet pulled your face forward as it went around and around and then twisted. I was okay on that ride until I ate a hot dog before and, well, just imagine what happened. The people below were touched a little bit. Remember the amazingly fast motorcycle barrel rider? Oh, how about the infamous Scrambler that darted in and out and threw you from side to side? There was so much fun as a kid at the fair! Candy apples, cotton candy, hot dogs, french fries; it was just a wonderful experience with friends and family!

Important Life Lessons I Gleaned from Growing Up in Waycross

- I learned that next to our family, friends are vitally important; and there is nothing like having a good friend.
- I learned that if we ask the question, "How are you doing?" it is important to pause and listen to their answer.
- I learned that this life goes by rather fast, and we need to take time to smell the roses or the aroma of the coffee.
- I learned that a place of worship or the place you connect with other people is what helps keep this country glued together and gives us sanity.
- I learned we will often be surprised what we can learn from others when we take time to listen to them.
- I learned that people are valuable. And when they are treated with value, respect is returned.
- I learned that all men and women are our teachers; take time to give them a listening session.
- I learned that three words can make a difference: I Love You.
- I learned that a house is not a home. They who live in the house create the home.
- I learned that life changes, plans change, and change is not all bad.
- I learned that it is good to be somewhat flexible.
- I learned that nothing on this earth is permanent—not a house, not a car, not a yard, not stuff.
- I learned that many things I wanted, once I got them, I did not want them that much after all.

- I learned that we do not need to complain about what we do not possess but to be thankful for what we do possess.
- I learned that there are good people in every neighborhood; take time to know them.
- I learned that no matter how much money you have or do not have, giving is the key.
- I learned that if you have a job, you show up on time, work hard, and make your boss look good.
- I learned that my work experiences, for sure, outweighed my playtime experiences.
- I learned that we don't have too much time with the people we meet, so do not take them for granted; they may be here today and gone tomorrow.
- I learned that all people you meet desire to be appreciated no matter where they live.
- I learned that the people who were in your life when you were young were placed there for a purpose.
- I learned that we do not have to be intimidated by people; for no one is better than you, and you are not better than anyone.
- I learned that there will always be a missing link, and it needs to be filled; and only God can fill that void.
- I learned that having respect and honor for parents is a vital truth and principle in life to bring us the favor of God. The favor of God will open doors that no man can open.
- I learned that the older we get, the more we will desire to remember how it was back in the day.
- I learned, as I got older, that life sure goes by fast and to be sure to take time for your friends.

Summertime in the South

Every summer, for a few weeks, I would go stay with either my Aunt Willie in Surrency, Georgia, or my Aunt Mittie in Daytona, Florida. Now with which one would you rather go stay? Back in the day, it really did not matter, for either place was family! No doubt, those summer experiences probably helped me develop and mature in those early years. Surrency was located about fourteen miles from Baxley. It seemed like I spent a little more time there than in Daytona. However, when I was able to go, it was great going to Daytona! My cousin would take us to the beach, and we did have the opportunity to learn to surf; but it took more than a few days or even weeks to pick it up and get good at it. I can remember our going to the Daytona Speedway in July. I think it was the Daytona Firecracker 400! Those were some fun days!

When we headed to Surrency, we would always say, "We are going out in the country." Our family that lived there worked in the lumber business as well as the tar, tobacco, turpentine, cotton, and sugarcane industries. At some point, when growing up, I did do summer work in each of these businesses with my uncle and cousins. Stringing tobacco was not fun when it was one hundred degrees with no air conditioning. I do not know how they did it year after year. It was so hot. I guess if you never had air conditioning, you don't know what you are missing.

One of the worst summer memories was when my cousin said, "Let's go to the watermelon patch and eat some melon." We are talking hot watermelon. Have you ever eaten a hot melon on a sweltering day in the middle of a patch? Not fun afterward! During this mishap, there's watermelon everywhere—throwing it, smashing it, eating it; and it was all over us. Because we ate too much, it did not take us long to get sick, so we would then head to the little water hole just down from the old wooden house. We would take off our clothes, hit the water, get dressed, go home, and no one knew we had been to the watermelon patch!

Picking cotton was hard work. Luckily, I only recall having to work one summer in the cotton field. How about working the sugarcane? We would feed the mill the stalks of sugarcane as the mule would walk round and round, grinding it. There was a container attached to the mill that would collect the squeezed sugarcane juice. I will never, never forget what happened on one occasion. One of my cousins said, "Larry, let's drink some of that fresh sugarcane juice." We did; and truthfully, I believe we turned as green as the juice! I don't think I had ever been that sick! Moral: Don't do everything your cousins invite you to do! Now on the other hand, I do remember the smell of that sugarcane cooking to make syrup, and it was a great smell. Fresh syrup was the best!

For those of you that traveled on Sunday afternoons with your parents to visit your relatives, you can remember how long that ride seemed to be; it was like forever! It was, at the most, forty-five to sixty miles away, but it was just so long to get there and back in the day! Today, I can drive that same route and highway and get there in much less time; but that was just the way it was back then, wasn't it? That is right, that was how it was!

Lawless Living Was among Us

We are all made from dust and dirt, and no one should judge another. I will not mention any of my friends' names in this chapter; but on some occasions, some of us were living in lawlessness, and it would have consequences. What I mean is, from time to time, we forgot about the law and, almost every time, we would do something that we knew was wrong. Wrong thinking always creates wrong behavior! Isn't that true? By the way, a friend is always a friend; and we should always be there when a friend needs us, whether it be in the good, bad, or the ugly. Let's take a few minutes and walk down this memory lane together.

How about our behavior at the famous Waycross Drive-In? How about Clayton's Lake? How about the bowling alley? How about those famous clay pits? How about Your Night Out? I do remember we had some strong Christians in our class of 1970, and many of us probably kept our prayer lives busy. When a young man or young lady does not put Christ first in his or her life, no matter how much he or she attends church, wrong will manage to find a way to him or her. We are all sinners, and we find some amazing Bible verses that help us with our sinful condition. A few are the following: Romans 3:10, Romans 3:23, Romans 5:12, Romans 5:8, Romans 6:23, Romans 10:9–10, and Romans 12:1–2. Throughout my childhood, middle school, and high school years, I, for one, had no idea what these verses said or meant. So many of us just did not take time to consider the sinful nature we came into this world with and which controlled us. I think, from time to time, perhaps a few of our classmates may have tried to witness to me about Christ, but for some reason, my heart did not fasten on what they were trying to say. So in my own personal life, I remained in a lost condition without Christ as my Savior until I was twenty-one years of age. I will share more later about that amazing year, 1973, when my life changed from the inside out and for which I am truly thankful! If you are one of those that prayed for me or others in high school, please let me know, for I would love to personally express my gratitude to you! A sinner acts like a sinner; and sadly, so many of us lived as though there was no eternity. Lawless living will cause much pain and suffering for sure! So may I say, please know that when I share stories of "how it was" and "what we did," I am not glorifying wrong; I am only saying life "before Christ" can be a lawless one, which includes many hurts, habits, and hang-ups.

Lonely Night in Georgia

Let's go back to a few lonely, lawless nights. Allow me to give just one example of a horrific evening that I will never forget. Waycross was playing in Jesup for a big football game. Four of us guys decided to drive to the game in a 1963 green Chevrolet, three on the column, six-cylinder, four-door Impala. We were doing the wrong thing—yes, we were. We decided to get some alcohol, and off to the game we went. As we were driving home, we drove through Screven. There was a traffic light there, and we stopped as it turned red. As soon as the light changed to green, the driver hit the gas; and as he was shifting gears, somehow it happened. He threw the gear in reverse and dropped the transmission right there in the middle of the highway and right in front of the local jail. It was terrible! Here we were, all four of us in possession of booze and heading to that jail. It was horrible! We were so embarrassed! We had been so lawless! Our wrong thinking had caused wrong behavior! Each of us made our lonely, uncomfortable phone call to our parents. Soon they came to get us out, take us home, and the rest was history with discipline, punishment, and payback—absolutely not fun. If any kids are reading this, *do not* emulate our foolish behavior. That was a *lonely night in Georgia*! Moments like those may sound exciting and seem fun, but when your parents or friends have to come get you, it is a miserably lonely night!

What Was Your Favorite Family Car?

I recall a few favorites:

- The 1962 light-green Corvair with the engine in the back—I don't think that car lasted for a long time. It was not big enough for the family.
- The 1961 Ford Falcon was a great car—four-door, white, six-cylinder engine.
- I remember Dad brought home a brand-new, light-blue four-door Toyota, and we kept it one day; he said it was not big enough.
- Our family car, the 1962 black Buick Electra—wow, I loved it! It was fully automatic air-conditioning, tilted seats, great radio, and an automatic radio antenna. It had lots of buttons. The motor was strong, and you could squeal tires on black asphalt like crazy. But more than that, it was a great family car.
- My brother's 1956 red Chevrolet Impala was a real beauty with the shifter on floor. I appreciate my brother Ronnie taking time to teach me how to drive with the floor shift. It was so cool. I can remember it shifted so easily; he could shift it with his feet.
- My sister's 1963 VW Bug was light green with radio but no air-conditioning, but it would be so windy going down the highway with those windows open. Connie loved that car so much!

- I never owned a car until after I was drafted in the military and was stationed in Charleston. In 1975, I purchased a 1964 four-door Comet for $300.
- What was your favorite family car?

Special Times with Special Friends

- Swimming at the Holiday Inn Motel with friends was so much fun. The Willinghams owned the motel, and thanks to their daughter, Patti, we could all go swimming on a Saturday or Sunday afternoon.
- Patti had a bicycle built for two or better called two-seater, and she would let me borrow it on occasion. I would invite one of my friends to go along; and many times, we would ride a few miles out Central Avenue, come back, and go by the Dairy Queen for a vanilla cone dipped in chocolate, then we would clean up the bike and take it back to her house. She was such a dear friend and a sweet young lady!
- One summer, one of my high school friends, Doug, and I saved money from our jobs and took a full-week vacation to Daytona Beach. I am not sure how we pulled it off, but it must have been at the end of twelfth-grade summer break, just before college started. Doug drove his four-door, six-cylinder, dark blue Dodge. I believe it was also a three-speed on the column. That was a great week, and after our high school years, it was a fun, rewarding trip. That took some planning, and off we headed for a week in the sun! Doug later was in our wedding and has been a good friend for many years.
- One good friend was Rick. His family had a house on Jekyll Island, and it was always a pleasure to go down and stay over the weekend in their beautiful beach house—fun times at Jekyll! Rick was also the friend that would, in our senior year, drive across town and pick me up for school in

his new Super Beetle—one great car! That was the fastest car I had ever been in, but Rick was a great driver.

- Friday or Saturday nights driving around Waycross in either my dad's 1962 Buick or one of my friends' cars was a blast. All kinds of music were playing on the radio—songs like "Mr. Tambourine Man," "Traces," "(Sittin' on) the Dock of the Bay," and on and on. Any of us could name a song, and we would all join in the singing! How about "A Summer Place" by the Lettermen? Maybe a little "Turn! Turn! Turn!" or a few more by Connie Francis or Troy Donahue? Then there was a good one like "Georgia on My Mind" by Ray Charles. I think most people from Waycross loved the Swingin' Medallions and the Tams. I remember hearing over and over that well-known song "I've Been Hurt" by the Tams. You might even end the evening with good ole "Wipe Out" and hear that fantastic drum solo! How about the renown Four Tops singing "Ain't No Woman," Edwin Starr singing, "War," the Detroit Spinners' "Could It Be I'm Falling in Love," "I'll Be Around," or even "Rubber Band Man"? We are going back a little to remember the O'Jays singing, "Love Train," Diana Ross's "Ain't No Mountain High Enough," Smokey Robinson crooning "Cruisin'" or "Being with You." Remember the Temptations singing "Just My Imagination," the Three Degrees singing "When Will I See You Again," and lastly, Gladys Knight's iconic "Midnight Train to Georgia"? I am sure your mind is being filled right now with your favorite oldies but goodies! I am just saying, this is really how it was, and Waycross buzzed along with the music!
- Movies at the Ritz or the Lyric were always fun events with friends. When we were younger, for some reason, our mom made us dress up to attend the movies. I am not talking about like Halloween stuff but dress up in church clothes to go to the movie house! We would have, every now and then, a premiere showing in Waycross, and the sidewalk would be lined with people to buy their tickets. You never

know, something like that just might come back! I recall one Halloween when a special "happening" was taking place at the Lyric. It was the talk of the town! People were lined up days ahead to be a part of this big celebration. The event was a live feature of horror at the Lyric. I have never been so scared in my life as I was that night. I can remember someone stretched a wire across the theater and at a certain point, they released something down the wire, and it hit the back of our necks! You talk about screaming—never have I heard anything like that!

Summer of 1970

When I Began to Notice the Power of Feeling Lonely

Graduation was over! My close friends were going in different directions in life, such as college, military, or a job out of town. To my keenest recollection, the summer of 1970 was a bit lonely. I was working at Rivenbark's men's shop. That summer was busy with many of my friends coming in to buy new clothes to take to college in the fall. Valdosta State, Georgia Southern, Georgia College, South Georgia, University of Georgia, ABAC, Georgia Tech were the colleges I remember my friends going off to attend. The realization began to set in that our carefree high school days were now over, and we friends just may not see each other again for a long time. Well, that was true. Most of us have not seen each other since that summer. A few, I would see on occasion; but most of them, to this day, I have never seen again. But of course, we have many memories. Every now and then, I would take out the Turpicone yearbook and look through the pages to refresh my memory of those great people at Waycross High School. Years later, there have been forty to fifty of us that have stayed in contact in some way, mostly through social media. I am thankful for Facebook for, even in 2021, we are able to share thoughts, words, pictures, and memories with one another.

That fall, I stayed behind in Waycross to attend the University of Georgia off campus, and a few of my high school friends attended with me. Many of us did continue to get together, hang out, and have some fun times!

Off to Another City for College

O ne of my friends came home from Georgia College during the 1970 Christmas holidays and said, "Larry, you really should consider going to Georgia College in Milledgeville." Well, after much thought, after all the paperwork, and driving my brother's 1971 Pinto, I headed to Georgia College in the fall of 1971. Thanks to Nancy! That September morning, I checked in and got moved into Ennis Dormitory, which sat on a hill across from the main campus. That afternoon, I heard from Nancy who lived in Bell Dorm across the large front courtyard of the college. "Larry, I would like you go tonight to eat with some friends, and I have a blind date for you." What? I had not even unpacked yet! Nancy had already met a guy, and he happened to be my roommate. How did that happen so quickly? Long story short, my roommate and I picked the girls up on a street corner adjacent to the campus. Now we have four of us crammed in that little red Pinto, and off we went to Pizza Hut. My blind date's name was Ranée; she was a Decatur (Ga) High Bulldog, in her sophomore year at Georgia College. She was incredibly beautiful, with long brown hair, beautiful blue eyes, and a smile that would win your heart. The date ended up being very pleasant, and she welcomed me to Georgia College! I found out later how this unusual date all came to pass. Because I had the only available vehicle, I was needed. It had all been set up without my knowing it. Nancy had a date but needed a ride. Larry had the ride but needed a date! Ranée did not know the details either! Thanks, Nancy, for that surprise date, and thanks to my roommate for helping make it all come together! Ranée and I ended up getting married in 1974! We have been married for forty-seven years at this writing, and both of us realize vividly how God can use situations (that do not make sense) to bring two people together for a life journey! This life-changing night at GC strangely reminds me of an eighth-grade experience in which I was required to stand in class and quote a poem.

Poem "The Road Not Taken" by Robert Frost

The poem "The Road Not Taken" was the assignment due to be recited in the eighth grade. I recall how embarrassed I felt when I totally bombed it by forgetting the words and sat down with tears in my eyes. I am not sure what happened; my brain just seemed to freeze up. Did this ever happen to you? Absolutely! I think I said to myself, "Never again will I get up in front of people and speak!" The poem itself challenges readers to ponder the thoughts about choices we make in life. Should we go the mainstream or head in a different direction? Certainly, in this life journey, we all must make decisions regarding what is the best route to follow. No doubt, we all have regrets that a road we took on some occasion was not the right choice. As a result, each of us may breathe a heavy sigh over what "just might have been" in life. I look back over my life, and I do have regrets of not taking the path that could have offered a better opportunity; but I think each of us has done so. Would you agree?

A true assessment might be that the theme of "The Road Not Taken" concerns what did *not* happen in life. It is quite easy, when faced with a big decision, to choose the most popular one or the path of least resistance. But is it the best choice? We are, for sure, destined to go down one of the paths while perhaps regretting being unable to take them both. The bottom line: We may live our lives believing we have sacrificed one for the other. At some point, each of us has had that thought cross our mind. Was the choice made the most positive, most productive, and even the most prosperous? Truly, only time will tell!

I am so glad that the cross of Christ was made aware to me. And because I chose His cross, my life was changed forever! Now I desire to point as many as possible back to that amazing cross!

From a Dormitory to a Barrack

As a college student, my desire was to receive a degree in business administration. I dated Ranée my entire first year there at Georgia College. When summer break came, we both returned to our hometowns to work and spend time with our parents. I remember so vividly when the news came in midsummer that the final picks for the Vietnam war draft were soon to take place. Across the country, young men were glued to their television sets to see if their birthday might fall under the billet number 50. If it did, then off to war with Uncle Sam they would go!

Mine was number 38! I became a "chosen one"! There was a special program for a brief period of time that allowed anyone picked for the draft, if he so desired, to join another branch of the armed services. That being so, I made a choice to follow in my dad's and brother's footsteps to become a sailor in United States Navy!

In a few short months, I had loaded a plane in Jacksonville, Florida, and was headed to boot camp for military service. Company 332 at the Naval Training Center in San Diego, California, would be my next home, along with ninety-two other sailors. I remember, like it was yesterday, seeing the airplanes that would fly so close to the ground over the training center as I specifically thought of those flying back east like to good ole Georgia. It is amazing how homesick a person can become in boot camp! I fondly recall a forty-two-page letter (written in my absence, one page per day) that I received from that wonderful young lady I met at Georgia College on that famous blind date. Incidentally, it took about eight weeks for me to read that letter!

In Waycross, when I signed up with Fred, the navy recruiter, I chose the MOS (military occupation code) of dental technician.

Immediately after boot camp (after many trips to the medical infirmary with extreme sunburn from marching on the asphalt or concrete grinder), I attended the dental technician training school on Thirty-Second Street in San Diego. I look back and remember so many of my boot camp buddies and the other students in the training school. To this day, I stay in touch with a few of those great guys with whom I enjoyed the long weekends biking, camping, and exploring the beautiful San Diego Zoo and surrounding area.

Life was moving a bit faster now as my first duty station became Charleston, South Carolina. I had wished for Scotland, but that specific duty station was not available, so off to Charleston! That old city became a beloved and beautiful place to live.

This is where the message of "The Road Not Taken" began to become a little clearer. When I look back and remember the ten houses in which we had lived and the "for some reason" moments, some lessons learned as younger person began to make sense to me. For instance, because of my childhood training, I learned that I was no better than anyone, and no one was better than me; therefore, I did not have to battle too much with intimidation or comparison of myself to others. It is a great way to live! Truthfully, everyone who makes a new relationship can learn from that new person and hopefully picks up a few ideas that can help along the way. Judging others and speaking ill of others will cause a person to be stopped in his tracks.

Would I have loved to have finished college? Yes. Would I have loved to have received that business degree? Yes. But now was the time to move on and let some things go in life. I had a new chapter, a new journey, and many new people to meet. Life was taking a series of turns and rather quickly! I am now established in my new duty station and enjoying a new challenge to perform as a Dental Technician, for which I'd been well-trained. As I look back, I can see that the reason that I probably chose that specific naval vocation was that it was a direct reflection on the influence that I had received from Dr. Eleazar, our family dentist in Waycross. I always liked the way I was treated by Dr. Eleazar and the care I had received as a patient of his dental practice. It was as if a good seed had been planted in my mind or heart to somehow pursue the dental field. This was a good beginning!

Having gotten myself settled in Charleston, my life was about to take another big jump and an exceptionally good one! About two weeks before our wedding, one of my navy friends, Bob, shared with me about a new and special experience in his life. "Larry, this week, through the influence of a friend in Deland, Florida, I asked the Lord Jesus Christ to become my personal Savior. Larry, would you want to know if you died that you would go to heaven?" Of course, who would not want to know that? In a matter of minutes, after he explained from the Bible what he was talking about, I knelt down by my couch, and when I got up off my knees in my little apartment on that Friday afternoon in 1973, my life had an amazing, bright, forgiving, energetic, enthusiastic outlook! Wow, how awesome it felt to have all your sins forgiven and now to be given what is called the gift of eternal life. And I don't think the proper word was even invented yet! In just two weeks, Ranée and I were scheduled to be married, and everything was set to go! Oh, did I tell you? We were engaged in the parking lot of the famous Green Frog Restaurant in Waycross close to that giant frog structure.

I know this sounds terrible and not really romantic, but I had placed the ring in my sock for some reason! It took a moment to get it out of my sock, but when I did, I humbly asked Ranée to marry me. And the great news, she said, "Yes!"

Now that Ranée had graduated with her teaching degree, and I was settled in Charleston, it was time to begin another chapter. January 5, 1974 was a great day! We were married at Oakhurst Baptist Church in Decatur, Georgia. A few of my longtime Waycross friends were in the wedding, and I appreciated all they did to be a part of that special celebration!

Now, our new journey has begun! An apartment payment, power bills, water bills, more groceries, and all that goes with married life. You remember how it all changed, but it was a good change! Isn't it amazing how life can just take you down different roads? I can emphatically say I was so glad it was time to take *that* road! We discovered and soon joined Charleston Heights Baptist Church, a great church with a dynamic pastor whom we all called Brother Jay. What an amazing, evangelistic pastor he was who loved people and preaching the gospel! Under the influence of an authentic, friendly usher named Frankie, I saw the importance of the church-life community for a new Christian. One of the staff members took an interest in me and would spend hours teaching me the books of First and Second Timothy in the New Testament. Other friends came into our lives. Jay, Corky, Sam, Rose, Bill, Debbie, Johnny, Lynn, Bob, Judy, Debbie, Ricky, and so many others made an impact upon our lives. Years later, we have not forgotten them, and amazingly, we all have stayed friends over the years. The song goes, "A friend's a friend forever if the Lord's Lord of them." In most cases, that fact has played out in my life. Pretty soon into my new Christian journey, my eighth-grade comment about "never again getting up in front of people and talking" evaporated. I was being asked to get up in small groups and tell my life story. I would always start off with, "I lived in ten homes in ten years," and probably people got tired of me talking about those days, but that was a huge part of my life. In fact, that *was* my life! Next, I was being invited to speak to a few hundred people, and I was as nervous as I was in that junior high classroom! Thankfully, with the blessing of the Lord and His strength and grace, we did it!

Another powerful question: How can I have an impact on the lives of the other sailors who work with me at the dental clinic? Well, with Bob's (who led me to Christ) example and the energy being displayed by our arduous work, loyalty, and desire to be the best we possibly could be, we did not see it all; but other sailors were beginning to have a desire to see a change in their lives that they saw in ours. Pretty soon, Dave, Randy, Tom, and many other sailors were asking Jesus to save them and give them eternal life. We would now stand for weekly inspection on Wednesday, and out of forty sailors, seven of them had become new believers in Christ; and the revival began. Soon, we were being connected to other believers on the base. Our great usher-friend, Frankie, was a wonderful encouragement to bring the sailors to church; and it was genuinely like a *wave* had begun of seeing young men and women's lives experience a fresh start in life with new goals and new ambitions. The atmosphere was explosive as we were now witnessing a small revival, taking place on the naval base there in Charleston. Our church was growing; other churches were growing; and the energy was electric as we saw people's lives being transformed and their destinies changed forever through the power of God!

Something else began to happen! Some of my friends in Waycross got the word about what had happened in my life. As a result, one high school friend, Troy, asked Jesus to be his Savior. We are not talking about joining a church or getting baptized or anything like that, we are talking about recognizing that we all are sinners and that over two thousand years ago, *one* man, Jesus Christ, died, shed His blood on the cross of Calvary, and rose from the dead. Yes, that *one* man can change the destiny of any human being. My dear buddy, Troy, called on the Lord to be his Savior, and many other friends wanted to know the difference that Christ could make in their lives. My heart is thrilled to know that so many of our high school and college friends are confident that they also will be spending all eternity with Christ the Lord! That knowledge should thrill us all!

Most of my friends back in the day called me Bullard. I like that name, my heritage, and the opportunities it has afforded me. You can take our amazing Creator of the universe, add His name to yours, and discover yourself going down roads you never thought you'd travel! Without a doubt, God can take the good, the bad, and the ugly and make something beautiful. One day, we will all leave this earth. Take some time to prepare for your next journey to a place called heaven. Trust Christ to be your personal Savior. Be good to people; we do not know what they are going through, and they just might need *you* to be their friend.

While still serving in the navy, I was approached by our pastor, Brother Jay, who asked me to become a part-time, then later full-time, youth pastor at Charleston Heights. After my four years with Uncle Sam were up, I went off to Bible college, received a degree in pastoral leadership, and was given the honor to travel almost all the United States teaching and preaching the gospel of Christ. I do not take for granted the people that I have met in this life. I am grateful for the fact that God is bigger than any problem any of us might have and that He has placed each of us in His heavenly GPS system, knowing our needs and desires. May you know how much you are loved! The testimony I give now, after these many years, is one of gratitude and thankfulness for those teachers in school, friends in school, friends in college, friends in those many neighborhoods, friends in the workplaces, my precious wife, our four incredible children, their spouses, and those sweet nine grandchildren! How good God is! How grateful am I!

My wife and I have had the opportunity to be involved in church life for over forty-seven years, and the experience has been one of both mountain highs and valley lows. We have learned there really is no way to escape the effect of this earthly cosmos with its trials, tribulations, and tests! But we have learned the faithfulness of our great God, who promises to never leave nor forsake us! We have heard amazing stories of people in ministry that have touched the lives of hundreds and thousands and have enjoyed meeting many of these wonderful people. Every person you meet has something in his or her life to learn from, and the people you meet will also learn a few things from you.

Throughout the years, we have served in the Christian community as a youth director, house parents for an outreach house for wayward girls, assistant pastor, senior pastor, church planters, evangelism, and missions. Our ways have crossed with people that desired to do hurricane crisis projects, building projects, street ministries, youth camps, youth conferences, and one-on-one discipleship. We have been blessed to see hundreds and thousands of people come to know Christ as their Savior, and that has been the thrill of our lives! Just to see one more person ask Christ into their life causes not only the angels in heaven to rejoice, but it causes me to rejoice as well!

Have you accepted Jesus as your Savior? He is a gentleman and would never force Himself upon you; it is strictly your decision to make. But upon the cross of Calvary, He paid the penalty of sin for each of us and is waiting, with arms extended, for each of us to simply trust Him for salvation. If you'd like to invite Him into your life, simply pray something like this:

> Dear Jesus, I know that I'm a sinner and
> that I should go to hell for my sin. I believe You

died and rose again from the grave for my salvation. I'm asking You now to forgive all my sin and take me to heaven when I die. Thank You for saving me. Help me to live for You! Thank You for saving my soul today, _____ *(today's date)*. In Jesus' name, I pray. Amen.

A Lifelong Friend

Years later, when we were in the middle of fulfilling our careers and callings in life, my wife and children would join me in travels from city to city across America, speaking and singing in youth camps and conferences. One of my good friends in high school, Dave, called me one day and said, "Larry, can you drive up to Charlotte and bring your wife?"

The next day, we were there with him. Dave took us to a Dodge/Plymouth car dealership and said, "I want you to pick out a vehicle, and I want to buy it for you."

We said, "What!"

He sure did. It was a brand-new Town and Country minivan, big enough to accommodate my family of six. I could not believe it! God had blessed him greatly in his business, and he wanted to be a blessing to us. I have told him many times; but again, may I say, "Thank you, Dave!"

Taking What I Have Learned
to Corporate America

After serving in the church for many years, I began to ask the Lord to expand my territory and to open opportunities to share life principles with the corporate world. In 2008, during the financial crisis in America (you remember, I am sure), that door we had prayed about opened! We were hosting a seminar on excellent customer service, and the main speaker was extremely pleased with the customer service that our own staff was offering to participants at the event. After the seminar, I was asked to consider traveling and sharing with the corporate world what I had learned through the years about customer service. I honestly was shocked that this was really happening! I then remembered asking the Lord to do this very thing.

After some basic training and learning the logistics of the company, I found myself loading a plane and traveling from one city to the next, teaching and training corporations and companies in public and in onsite seminars about excellent customer service, along with many other topics of interest. My mind took me back to the grocery business, peanut business, clothing business, and the many things I had seen, heard, and learned from those that had gone before me. Certainly, our foundational years can allow any of us to launch creative ideas for the future! This is one reason I encourage young people to stay teachable and meek and to ask more questions than trying to give answers. Life is filled with so much opportunity!

It is very humbling to walk in a room full of people desiring to learn and to progress in their area of expertise. It is my job to do my best to empower them, and I am so honored that these people would come, sit, and learn from this guy. What a blessing!

Principles about Life I Learned from Others through the Years

Here are some wonderful truths that have been passed down to my generation that I have found most helpful. (I wish I could say they have always followed these principles; but we all make mistakes. And trust me, I have made my share.)

- Purpose to be a problem solver rather than a problem creator.
- Believe in what you are doing.
- Go where the people are to meet their need.
- Take ample time to plan.
- Realize you do not have to close every deal to be successful, just some of them.
- Recognize, you have some attributes that can benefit others.
- Know that others have traits you can emulate.
- Do not spend much time with your critics.
- Realize, timing is important in every endeavor.
- Respect authority.
- Do not discriminate.
- Spend some time developing passion for your vocation.
- There is a right time and a wrong time to approach people with your idea.
- Spend time mentoring others, and educate them as much as they'll allow.
- Do not judge people by their outward appearance.
- Know that if you really want something, you need to take steps to get it.

- Know your worth, your value, and the same for others.
- It is vital that you do not try to succeed alone; it takes others involved in your life.

Unique Opportunities

O ne of the highlights of traveling and speaking in seminars was the opportunity to spend a few days holding a training seminar entitled "Communicating with Tact and Professionalism" at one of our country's NASA space centers. After a detailed background check that I had never experienced, I found myself standing in front of a few hundred people, teaching and conveying creative ideas that had been passed down to me from leaders who knew much, much more than I did!

To be honest, I was a bit startled at the opportunity and, for sure, humbled that, in my mind, a little guy like me could be presented with such an amazing privilege. I guess one thing I have learned in this life is that God knows where we are and what He has placed in us. We are all designed for His purpose in this life. I truly believe what I am sharing here with you. If you have not found purpose yet, spend some time reading the Bible and asking your heavenly Father for direction. For real, *He* will lead you down paths and allow you to be discovered! You will never have to force God's plan. *He* has you in mind!

Once, as I stood on the platform at a Fortune 500 event where hundreds of people were in attendance, a sudden fear came all over me. "I cannot go out there. What do I have to say that these people would want to hear?" When I was introduced (and I am not sure how fast these thoughts rolled through my brain), I saw myself standing up in the eighth grade, doing my best to quote "The Road Not Taken" and remembering the fear that had overwhelmed me. Well, thankfully, in this circumstance, the results were much different, for I now had a personal relationship with Christ, and the scripture was saying, "God has not given me the spirit of fear, but love, power, and a sound mind." I quoted that verse, bowed my head for faith not fear, love, nothing less, and power to influence other people for good. I found out later, there were not hundreds but thousands of people in attendance that night. Truly, with the promises of God, you and I can accomplish anything God calls on us to do; and that is rather awesome!

From 2008 to 2019, my heartbeat was to do my best to empower people—all people—from every segment of life. I went on to write a manual entitled "Life Principles for Leaders." I can testify to the fact that years of preparation can create opportunities to influence people!

Maximum Life Impact

In what season of life are you presently living? One of the most powerful tools each of us owns is our tongue. We can use our tongue to speak life to people, or we can speak death to people. Years ago, I made a decision to do my best to use my tongue to speak life and to focus on edifying, encouraging, and exhorting people from all walks of life.

Now in my older years, it is my great desire to point as many people as possible to Christ, God's Word, family, patriotism, and do my very best to make a maximum life impact, whether it is with our children, grandchildren, family members, friends, or the person we just met in a restaurant. I am sure that you who are reading these words feel the same way and have a desire to make a maximum life impact as well!

You and I can make the difference! Think about the season of life you are in, and set out to be the difference. Someone needs you. You need someone. We all need one another!

Missions

Our most recent endeavor in ministry has been to travel overseas to teach and train missionaries in their native lands for the work of the ministry. One unique experience just took place just a few months ago! My son and I were invited to travel with two other men to Nigeria to empower over two thousand students in the *ways* of the Lord. That experience, while fraught with some uncertain and dangerous moments, was incredible! Loving God and loving people will open doors that no man can shut! Soon afterward, the invitation came to spend some time in South Africa to teach and train a wonderful group of men and women in the area of creative leadership.

Another passion I have is to help victims of hurricanes, storms, and tornadoes within our land. God has blessed us with many friends that share this same passion; and together, we call all make a difference. When Hurricane Katrina hit Louisiana and Mississippi, leaving thousands without food, shelter and clothing, I was able to lead a group of men and women to serve and adopt a community that had lost it all. With just a little courage, faith, and cooperation, this small yet willing group went the second and third mile to help others! God bless those faithful servants! God bless America, and God bless Americans!

Epilogue

There is something special about growing up in a small town, especially a Southern city. And may I say, there was something very special about growing up in *Waycross*! Each of us can remember how it used to be and wonder how it is now.

College life followed high school; then military life took me way across the country for sure! Married life came in 1974, and on the horizon was another college near Chicago for ministry training. Soon, three precious children were born into the family. Wow, life seemed to be moving at a rapid pace since I had left Waycross! Living near Metro Chicago, I witnessed cultural changes, gained new perspectives, and was exposed to a whole different world than that of sleepy South Georgia! It is rather amazing. No matter how stimulating or exciting your current situation, if you've left your hometown with great memories, you always want to go back and see the people and places and have chats with a faithful few.

From the Chicago area, the trek took us to Texas to a small southeastern town near the Gulf of Mexico. Five years and one more precious baby later, an invite came for us to work in the North Augusta, South Carolina, to Augusta, Georgia, area—yay, back in Georgia again! Years passed, we would still manage to find our way back to Waycross to visit, journal, remember, ride around to see all the houses, and simply enjoy back-in-the-day conversations. On one occasion, my heart was so full, I sent an article of memories to the *Waycross Journal-Herald*, and they published it.

I hope my perspective on *Growing Up Where the Ways Crossed* will bring back memories for you and ignite cherished forever conversations with your friends and family. Let us never forget where we came from and who helped us along life's pathway. Waycross was a great place to grow up, and I have much admiration for those who stayed, worked, progressed, and helped to keep Waycross alive and well. A big thank-you to so many. You have made a difference. Salt is a preservative, and so many of you have been salty!

This writing is full of stories and episodes that I experienced firsthand, and I have shared them from Florida to New York to Los Angeles, whenever the opportunity arose. I found out that so many people love to hear stories of what it was like to grow up in a small city. It does not matter in what part of the country you grew up; there is just something about a smaller town or city and the way things were done. I also think it is very enlightening for those from smaller towns to be inquisitive and learn from those who originate from the big city as well. It is a great joy and honor to meet people from every pocket across our wonderful land that we call America!

One of my goals in life has been to write a book about growing up in Waycross and to share some my experiences with you, the reader. Thank you for taking time out of your schedule to read these words written with *you* in mind! I hope you jotted down your remembrances in the margins. I am sure you can make a list, very similar to my memories, of the places where you grew up; and if you ever want to author a book, it would be an honor to take time to read your life journey! Don't you think, if we put all our memories together, we could write a complete encyclopedia! Absolutely!

A Final Word

I would point any reader to the Waycross-Ware County Chamber of Commerce for detailed information and accuracy about Waycross itself, its origin, attractions, events, and significance. Many great articles have been written about the history of the city, and some are exceptionally good. One such article relates that the streets were designed in the pattern of the Maltese cross, the same eight-pointed cross worn by firefighters across our nation. We also read in the history of the city that someone traveling with the railroad gave Waycross its name "where the ways crossed" because of the railways that crisscrossed throughout the city. And another traveler declared that the city is "the way of the cross" because of the many churches that were built during its formative years. For me, all the claims are major factors in my life application.

The first two-thirds of this book are dedicated writings and episodes about where the ways crossed in my life experiences, and the final one-third is written concerning the way of the cross in my personal life. In *Growing Up Where the Ways Crossed*, I did not refer to the railroads but to the ways, paths, and the people I crossed as a child and youth. These agents had a direct impact on my life. And of course, upon discovering the liberating way of the cross, I experienced the greatest impact of all: my soul's salvation!

We all recall hearing or making the statement, "Our ways crossed." That remark always refers to a specific place. It was my boundless joy to share with you how our many ways may have crossed in this wonderful city of only fourteen thousand known as Waycross.

About the Author

For over forty-eight years, William Larry Bullard has used his keen eye, quick wit, and God-given wisdom to encourage people from all walks of life. As he ministers to others, he desires to have a maximum life impact and is most satisfied when given the opportunity to share life principles that have helped shape and sustain him during both lean and prosperous times. He shares his love of people and of God with his wife of forty-seven years, Ranée, as well as their four awesome children and nine beautiful grandchildren. It is his sincere hope that his readers are uplifted, inspired, and heartened for their very best days which lie ahead. His life verse, Psalm 19:14, best describes the desire of his heart: "Let the words of my mouth, and the meditation of my heart, be acceptable in thy sight, O Lord, my strength, and my redeemer."

William Larry Bullard, a native of Waycross, Georgia, graduated in 1970 from Waycross High School, the home of the Bulldogs. He attended the University of Georgia off campus, Georgia College, and later received a bachelor of science degree in pastoral theology from a midwestern Bible college. He has been active in ministry-related endeavors for forty-five years, serving as youth director, youth conference speaker, assistant pastor, Christian college vice president, as well as senior pastor. In addition, Larry founded Life Group Seminars designed to teach and train men and women in their skill paths. Presently, Larry continues to speak in corporate seminars, revivals, conferences, retreats, and overseas mission projects.

CPSIA information can be obtained
at www.ICGtesting.com
Printed in the USA
LVHW041519110522
718479LV00017B/56